THE STORY OF

Victor F. **Weaver** ®

"Nobody Knows Chicken Like the Folks at Weaver!"

BY ALLAN W. SHIRK

The Story of Victor F. Weaver, Inc.
"Nobody Knows Chicken Like the Folks at Weaver!"

by Allan W. Shirk

Library of Congress Number: 2020922309
International Standard Book Number: 978-1-60126-710-8

Masthof Press
219 Mill Road | Morgantown, PA 19543-9516
www.Masthof.com

Table of Contents

CHAPTER 4
CHANGING DIRECTION:
THE WHOLESALE MARKET, 1950-1960s

CHAPTER 5
THE PUERTO RICO CONNECTION

CHAPTER 6
THE ERA OF PREPARED FOODS,
1970-1980s

CHAPTER 7
AMONG GIANTS:
THE CRESTING WAVE OF THE 1980s

CHAPTER 8
LEGACY

Acknowledgements

I want to acknowledge and thank all who have become part of this work in so many ways. Your information and stories have given life to this effort.

I want to thank Janet and Larry Newswanger for their support and information about the Weaver family and business. They were a constant source of information and encouragement along the way. Irene Martin Weaver gave insightful information about her husband, Dale Weaver. The extended Weaver family members of the United Service Foundation provided me with a good beginning to this story with their reminiscences at Camp Hebron in Halifax, Pennsylvania.

As I was nearing completion of my first book about inventor Edwin B. Nolt, Merle Good shared some insights about writing. He encouraged me to decide when a work is finished and then to quit. When he asked what my next book would be about, I had no response as I just wanted to finish my first book. As I handed a copy of the finished Nolt book to my friend, Delbert Seitz, he said, "You should do a book on Victor Weaver." He worked for Victor and admired his business ethics. Months later, Phyllis Pellman Good opened that window of curiosity further as she made me aware of Victor's involvement in beginning the Spanish Mennonite Church in New Holland, Pennsylvania.

Thank you to Margaret High for all her suggestions and faithful editing.

Donald Horning soon became a part of the project, making the resources of the New Holland Area Historical Society available. His help and knowledge of the area were useful. Resources of the Lancaster Mennonite Historical Society were especially helpful regarding settlement of the Weaverland Valley and Weaver family roots.

Melvin S. Mitchell was a faithful source of information I could turn to during most of this writing. His story of growing along with the company from his teenage years resonates with Ben Burkholder's similar experience of being there at the beginning of Weaver Poultry and becoming a part of the emerging management team for many years. His unpublished writing provided by his daughter, Brenda Burkholder, was a valuable part of the early story. Thanks also to Bill Pellman who shared about his early experiences at Weaver.

My thanks to Allon H. Lefever and Keith Stuckey, who were part of the second generation professional management group. They provided valuable insights into the struggle as Dale Weaver's team pondered the company's future in the 1980s.

Thanks to the following whose photographs add interest to the narrative: Lester Blank, Larry Brown, Roy S. Burkholder, Francisco Jr. and Arlene Delgado, Miriam Frey, Tina Hess Glanzer, Michael Good, Carol E. Kauffman of WellSpan Philhaven, Lancaster Mennonite Historical Society, New Holland Area Historical Society, Larry and Janet Newswanger, Joanne Siegrist, Keith Stuckey, and Glenn Weaver.

Thank you to those who provided valuable information through interviews and phone conversations. Their names appear in the Works Cited pages. They were a major source of information and inspiration for which I am grateful.

Foreword

In the later years of the nineteenth century, New Holland, Pennsylvania, was a typical, small town in eastern Lancaster County. The economy depended upon agriculture and its supporting businesses, but growth had slowed. Local leaders hoped incorporating the town in 1895 as a borough would attract industry and increase employment. Two important industries moved into the town's void: The Storb Silk Mill (later the Ix Silk Mill) and the New Holland Machine Company.

Pursuit of non-farm employment was still in place when Victor and Edith Weaver moved their small but growing poultry processing business from Blue Ball to New Holland in 1937. The move was immediately synergistic. Their company would become one of the county's major employers. In addition to Weaver, the New Holland Machine Company and Zausner's Cheese plant were all agricultural-related industries.

The Weaver story was some 20 years along when I became involved. My family's business supplied Weaver with fleet trucks and cars. Doing business with Weaver's was as much a relationship as it was business. A long-time Weaver employee told me that working at Weaver's felt like working with family. Doing business with Weaver's had a similar feeling.

As Victor Weaver and his son Dale gave leadership to their growing company, they recognized the importance of a vibrant community as beneficial to both. Their generosity enriched the community in numerous ways and made it more attractive to a growing labor force.

A few years ago, the Weaver family saw fit to place the story and artifacts of Victor F. and Edith M. Weaver and their business in the New Holland Area Historical Society Museum. In my role as a volunteer there, I was involved in putting together a yearlong exhibit featuring Victor Weaver and the Weaver's business story. This exhibit remains the most visited to date. It is a testament to the impact this organization had on its employees, New Holland and the surrounding area.

The question remains to be answered by future historians: Is the Weaver story and others like it from the last century still being replicated? Or are small towns and entrepreneurial businesspersons growing in tandem a thing of the past? Either way, this story is an important one to be preserved for the ages!

Donald Horning
New Holland Area Historical Society

Introduction

The summer before my junior year of high school, I worked at Victor F. Weaver, Inc. in New Holland. His poultry processing plant was just a few miles up the road from my East Earl home. I worked in the Cut-up Department. One of the final operations for us at the end of this disassembly line was to tear the backs of chickens from between the legs.

In the summer of 1958, I remember comparing my first paycheck with a friend as we stood on a loading dock at the plant. At that moment, Benjamin Burkholder, an important figure in Weaver management and also my Sunday School teacher, joined our conversation. I still remember what he said as he paused briefly, "Hey fellows, may I give you a bit of advice? What you're doing isn't a good idea." Some have described the company at Weaver as a family. In that spirit, big brother Ben shared his wisdom with the newly hired help before moving on to larger responsibilities.

At summer's end, I was glad to leave the cut-up room behind, never dreaming that one day I would sit at a computer to recount the Weaver story. This work began a few years ago after I gave a copy of my first book, *Ed Nolt's New Holland Baler*, to a friend; he encouraged me to consider writing about Victor. As an employee who worked personally with Victor, he was impressed with Victor's ability to integrate his business life and his faith. This was evident in his interaction with people and how he treated his employees. My own Weaver heritage and identity with the Weaverland Valley also drew me to this story.

As an innocent teenager, I had no idea what decisions were being considered in the front office, or what it might take to keep this local business thriving. How does a family grow its business, and keep its identity and values intact in such a competitive world? Must a business continue to get bigger to survive? What does one do with financial success that can inflate the ego and insulate one from the realities of the less fortunate? How does one pass on a business to the next generation? However, one question was settled in Victor's mind long before this: He simply tried to follow God's calling to be a Christian man running a business.

After years of successful growth, the Weaver company encountered the rough waters of business mergers and consolidation in the 1980s. It was unlike any problems confronted in the past. The struggle to become a national poultry contender with the giants of the industry fell short, and ownership of the company passed into the hands of others. Some would see this as failure but the spirit of "this beautiful company," as one described it, endures in the ongoing support of programs still benefitting many communities.

Allan W. Shirk

CHAPTER 1

Victor and Edith Weaver

WEAVER FAMILY ORIGINS

Victor's family roots were deeply established in Weaver history traceable to the early Weberthal settlement, later known as Weaverland, and first settler, Henry Weber. Four Weber brothers, John, Henry, Jacob and George, left their Switzerland homeland for a new life in Pennsylvania. Jacob arrived first and found his way to the Pequea settlement. Henry, John, and George came a bit later in 1718. By 1721, Henry was exploring the rich bottom lands east of Hans Groff's settlement and applied for 3,000 acres of land.

The three Weber brothers requested a legal survey of the land in 1721. When they learned their good friend and neighbor, David Martin, was coming from Switzerland, they purposely arranged for a vacant strip of land about a half mile wide and over a mile long in a straight line between Henry and Jacob's properties. They applied for a grant claiming the land for Martin in 1726. Upon his arrival the following year, David took possession of this new claim settling among his good friends and neighbors.

Historian Martin G. Weaver wrote, "In the spring of 1723, Henry, Jacob and George moved to the rich bottom lands between what is now Blue Ball and the Conestoga [river]. John Weber did not join this new venture. He remained in the Pequea colony. A congregation of

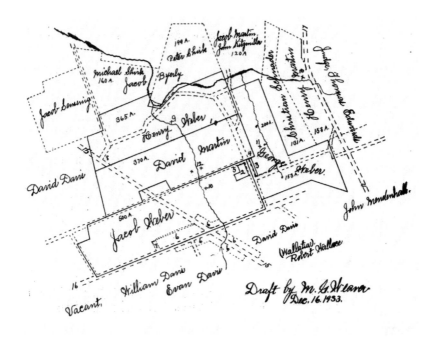

M. G. Weaver's draft of Weaverland Valley landholdings. Courtesy of Lancaster Mennonite Historical Society.

Mennonite brethren, centering in that section was soon formed for the worship of God . . ." Provisions were also made to begin a school in the community. By 1933 the land was divided into 45 farms.[1]

The original boundary line between David Martin and Henry Weber's properties intersects the Weberthal Cemetery diagonally, taking a triangle of land from each farm. A large headstone gives recognition to Henry Weber as "first settler. He married Maudlin Kendig, daughter of Jacob Kendig. Her grandfather, Martin Kendig, was among first Pequea settlers."[2]

Today the early settlers' graveyard sits in the middle of farmers' fields. From the graveyard, one can look southeast about a quarter of a mile away to two Mennonite meetinghouses. Separated by State Road 897 and theological differences, the Weaverland Mennonite Church of Old Order Mennonites sits on the crest of a small hill, across the road and below it is the Weaverland Anabaptist Faith Community.

M. G. Weaver hoped to preserve this small enclosure known as the Settlers' Grave-yard. The Weaverland Anabaptist Fellowship Church can be seen in the distance just right of farm buildings. The Old Order Weaverland Mennonite Church is on the crest of the hill beyond the farm buildings right of center. Author's photo.

In his booklet about the settlers' cemetery, Martin G. Weaver expressed his hope that preservation of this pioneer graveyard's "sacred soil," would increase respect for the memory of those who made it possible for their descendants to enjoy "the peaceful, quiet, prosperous Christian communities here and elsewhere." He concluded:

> *Within this small enclosure the dust of the earth mingled with the mortal remains of the first white settlers of the beautiful vale known and remembered as "Weber's" "'Thal,'" Weavers' Dale. Now Weaverland since the organization of the first Mennonite congregation by that name in 1730." Earl Union School was later established on land from the Henry Weber plantation.*[3]

Raymond and his brother Victor connected with that ancestral respect in 1981 as they updated their father's genealogical research going back to Henry and Maudlin Weber. Victor's middle name, Francis, was likely chosen in honor of fifth-generation Francis B. Weaver. At the time of this writing, the title to the original Henry Weber homestead has remained in the family since its 1723 founding.[4]

A brief note in the genealogy states that Francis B. Weaver and his wife, Magdalena Musser Weaver, started housekeeping on a farm along the "Conestoga creek" a short distance from Henry Weber's original homestead. The house, located "west of Weaverland stone quarry," was dismantled in 1980 as Martin's Quarry expanded.[5]

Many Weaverland families demonstrated similar rootedness and continuity, remaining on, or close to the land of their ancestors. Like many families in the community, Victor and his siblings got their eighth-grade education in the one-room Earl Union School their father, David H. Weaver, and grandfather, Harry M. Weaver, attended. Grandfather Harry was said to be known as "Gentleman Harry." Some said that he enjoyed taking his fine horse and buggy on trips to New Holland.[6]

DEATH AND MARRIAGE

Victor's mother, Cora Heller Weaver, died of diphtheria in 1932 when she was only 42 years old. She left six children and her bereaved husband behind. At 19, Victor was the oldest of the six children with Raymond, Ruth, Etta, Susie and Martin following him in birth order.

Years later, Martin preserved his vivid memories of his mother's death. He remembered it this way. On June 27 his mother got a sore throat. They saw Dr. Wenger in Terre Hill. Members of the family took turns giving Cora small amounts of whiskey with the hope that it would help clear her airway. Raymond, the last to do this, felt somehow he had failed her when she passed two days later on July 2.

Burial had to be done within 36 hours. Early the next morning neighbors and grandparents gathered to help plan the funeral. They met outside since a 30-day quarantine prevented their meeting indoors, or later visitations with the family. The funeral was held on Sunday afternoon, July 3, at the Weaver home. The family stood on the porch, and the preachers stood in the yard with those who gathered.

Martin wrote about the walk to the gravesite in the Weaverland Cemetery: "When I walked to the grave, I could hardly put one foot in front of the other." Although there's no record of Victor's thoughts of that day, it was likely a formative event in his life that helped to shape his sensitive, caring spirit. His younger brother's memories give us an idea of Victor's life in his childhood years.

The Fourth of July, the day after the funeral, was traditionally the first day of the Weaver's wheat harvest. The children watched as their father hitched three horses to the wheat binder to begin the harvest. That day he cut about 12 acres of wheat. One can only imagine the grief and many other emotions churning in his mind as he drove his horses. How would the family go forward?

Ruth was sixteen years old when diphtheria took their mother's life. It also took Ruth's teenage years as she assumed responsibilities for the household with some help from her younger sister, Etta. She gave leadership to holding things together at home until their father would marry again. But this troublesome time didn't rob Ruth of her sense of humor. Years later, she enjoyed teasing brother Victor that she deserved most of the credit for his business success.[7]

Life on the Weaver farm involved a lot of hard work done with horses and few conveniences. The children began working while quite young. At age 8, Martin was carrying water to the chickens and gathering eggs. When he was 10, he climbed up into the silo to throw down silage for the steers and cows. Water for the farm animals and to cool milk cans had to be pumped by hand. Later, a well and electric pump took over these arduous duties.

Martin soon learned his work wasn't done when he finished his chores. His father nicknamed him "house sitter," because he retreated into the house without checking if there was additional work to be done. He soon got the message. There was usually something else that needed to be done.

Cold winter days offered little comfort at home. There was no central heating system for the entire house. Second-floor bedrooms were frigid on cold winter nights. There was no heat, storm windows, or insulation. The rope bed and chaff bag mattress did little to insulate the boys from the cold even as they piled on more covers. Raymond and Martin experienced additional grief one cold night when the rope holding their mattress broke and tumbled them out on the floor. There was no recourse: They had to scramble from beneath the covers and mend the rope!

Earl Union School was about a half mile walk from home. The school had no electricity, no inside toilets, and no well. Water had to be carried from a nearby farm. A coal furnace in the back of the room heated the building. Every fall smell of the newly oiled floor greeted students on the first day of school.[8]

A Collection of Stories

From the Life of

Martin H. Weaver

As written by Martin H. and Vera B. Weaver
And paraphrased by Glori L. Brubaker

Victor's younger brother Martin H. Weaver's memories provide some insights into what young Victor's life at home might have been like. Courtesy of Larry and Janet Newswanger.

David Weaver married Katie Brubaker in 1935. She blended in well with the family and her role as the stepmother to the six children. Victor would soon leave home to begin his own life as a married man.

EDITH AND VICTOR

He married Edith Martin in 1936. They had known each other most of their lives. They attended the same church and were in the same Sunday School class much of that time. They began life together on a farm in the Blue Ball area. Edith's sister, Irene, married Ivan M. Martin a few years prior to her younger sister's wedding. Victor and

Ivan, now brothers-in-law, had similar values and interest in business. Ivan's business success would come from managing his stone quarry and New Holland concrete businesses. For Victor, the future would involve chicken.

Victor and Ivan were unusual men who recognized their wives as partners in their business endeavors. Irene Martin was more outspoken than her sister Edith, but both played significant roles in their husbands' businesses. When pondering decisions after Irene's death years later, Ivan would often comment, "I wonder what Irene would say."

It was unusual for husbands of that time to include wives in their business dealings, but Edith was part of the business from day

Edith and Victor with their young children, Janet and Dale. Courtesy of the Newswanger family.

South Custer Avenue, the site of the Weavers' expanding Weaver Poultry business in this building sometimes referred to as "the shed." Courtesy of the Newswanger family.

Janet and Dale play in their sandbox. Victor's 1946 Hudson pickup can be seen in the background. Courtesy of the Newswanger family.

one. Victor recognized her abilities, and she was an asset to the company. She was always on the payroll. Daughter Janet remembers hearing her parents' business conversations at home as a natural part of family life.

The Weavers' early success marketing 17 chickens at Sharon Hill soon made their kitchen inadequate. Leaving their Blue Ball farm, they moved to a property on South Custer Avenue in New Holland, Pennsylvania, where they began their business as Weaver Poultry.

The Weavers lived next to their plant in New Holland so it was natural for Edith to become involved. When the company incorporated in 1946, she became the first secretary and assistant treasurer of the board. She was a good listener and sounding board for Victor. She was someone he could confide in and tempered Victor's perfectionist tendencies. [9]

Edith was involved with plans for new buildings and her suggestion that future buildings should include all facilities under one roof became a reality. She was a co-owner of the business and an employee. Employees could buy Weaver discounted products at the company store. One day Edith stopped to make some purchases, and the young clerk, not recognizing her, asked for employee identification. The store supervisor quickly intervened and spared both customer and clerk further embarrassment. Perhaps as Edith told this story later she had a good-natured chuckle. She had a great sense of humor, and when laughter began for her, it was sometimes difficult to stop. She was a hearty soul who worked hard, liked to entertain, and enjoyed people. [10]

Before their son Dale joined the company and began work on new products, it was Edith who did some experimenting with new chicken products in her kitchen. One of her projects was perhaps a forerunner of the popular Weaver deli chicken roll. She cooked chicken feet to create a gelatin and combined it with poultry meat and celery in loaf form.

Daughter Janet remembers their frequent after-dinner routine. Victor would head back to his office for some evening work. But this wasn't his domain alone. Edith and Janet soon followed. While Janet read or found things to play with, Victor worked and Edith was available to listen or just to be present with her husband. If there were troublesome conversations about the company, Dale and Janet rarely heard them. Janet does remember a conversation between her parents regarding a significant financial commitment they had made to the church and how they were going to honor it along with the financial demands of their business.[11]

Janet related a story about her mother that illustrates her sensitivity and inclusiveness of others. When Janet was consulting an attorney about a business matter, he told of a time years earlier when he was a member of the Philhaven Hospital board. The board was holding its annual retreat at Camp Hebron, and his wife went along reluctantly. Aware of how this newcomer might feel, Edith introduced her to all the wives and welcomed her into this circle of predominantly Mennonite women who knew each other well. After that first year, his wife looked forward to this event.

GONE FLY'N

After their move from the Blue Ball farm, the young couple had plenty of space for a good-sized garden at their Custer Avenue home. However, there was a price to pay with the expansion of their chicken processing plant. The garden they shared together began to shrink in size with each new building project, and as Victor became more involved in his business, he spent less and less time in the garden.

Edith lost her gardening partner completely when Victor took up flying lessons. He was convinced that in the near future, everyone would be traveling by plane, and he wanted to get ahead of the rush. The local New Holland airport added to his convenience. Now, as Victor flew over their garden, Edith could look up from her weed-pulling to realize she was indeed alone amongst the vegetables!

New Holland Airport near the Weaver home where Victor began learning to fly. Courtesy of the New Holland Area Historical Society.

Airplanes were one example of Victor's forward thinking, curiosity and inclination for the latest things—whether it was kitchen appliances, gadgets or new means of travel—they seemed to draw him in. Not all the new gadgets worked as well as anticipated. Victor bought a device to scramble eggs in the shell. When it arrived, he noticed its bent shaft and straightened it before inserting into his first trial egg. He soon realized its failure to work was due to his adjustments. Another new product that attracted Victor's curiosity was a new type of clothes iron. He bought Edith a roller-type clothes ironer with wide rollers similar to commercial equipment, but designed for use at home.[12]

TELEVISION

Victor's interest in new things even influenced him to push the boundaries of church rules. By the 1960s, the Lancaster Mennonite

Conference prohibitions against television ownership were being test-ed. Members who had televisions were often reluctant to share that information with others. Some kept it hidden away for family use only. The assassination of President John F. Kennedy was an event that added to a growing Mennonite audience and television owner-ship.

During an extended family gathering at a Weaver Sunday noon meal, table talk turned to Lee Harvey Oswald's recent death. Victor invited his unsuspecting guests to join him around his, until now, un-seen TV. They tuned in and saw a rebroadcast of the incident. Watch-ing this shooting by Jack Ruby was more shocking than Victor's new technology.[13]

"MAKING DO" WITH WHAT YOU HAVE

Extended family members learned more of Victor and Edith's views of wealth from their unspoken examples. A granddaughter's spouse was "shocked" to discover the modest size of the new Weaver house built in 1950 at Custer Avenue. The decor appeared quite sim-ple "for a millionaire!" Ten years later, when fashions had changed and the Weaver furnishings were out of date, the same spouse was puzzled that no redecorating had taken place. It took a while to realize and respect the unspoken value—there's no need to spend money unnec-essarily even if you can afford to!

Edith grew up in a family that couldn't afford much beyond necessities. Janet said they had to "make do" with what they had. Even though circumstances were different now, she didn't change. Janet ob-served that "keeping up with others wasn't important to her."

Victor's greatest indulgence was buying a new car almost every year. At first he drove Hudsons. After Hudsons were no longer being produced, he drove a Dodge or Chrysler. When he was ready for an-other new car, he wanted to give someone a good deal on his used car. He didn't try to get the highest dollar amount possible. He wanted to pass on a good car at a very reasonable price. This policy reflected his own manner of making decisions on major purchases. He would ask the price and then decide to buy or not. He didn't haggle. He also observed this practice when getting his yearly new suit. He either sold clothing like this very reasonably or gave it to others.[14]

An artist's rendition of the Weavers' new house on the left, built in 1950. Ben Burk-holder's family occupied their old house shown on the far right. Courtesy of the Newswanger family.

Victor stands in front of the Weavers' new home built in 1950. Courtesy of the Newswanger family.

CHAPTER 2

Birth of a Business:
The Market Era, 1937-1950s

SHARON HILL—TESTING THE WATERS

On a Saturday morning in 1937, several hours before dawn, Victor and his wife, Edith, made preparations for what became a significant day in their lives. They loaded 17 freshly dressed, ice-packed, whole chickens into the trunk of their car and set out for Sharon Hill Farmers' Market in the suburbs of Philadelphia. Perhaps they worked late into the evening finishing their work at the kitchen sink on their Blue Ball farm. How much time had the task taken, and what thoughts flashed through their minds as they worked? These chickens, a small amount in retrospect, represented a significant amount of work to be done in the Weavers' home. To kill, de-feather and eviscerate what seemed like a small amount of poultry in hindsight, might have been enough midway through the operation in that busy kitchen to give this young couple pause—what had they gotten themselves into![1]

Victor's first business experience with chickens involved work for his uncle, Harry H. Weaver Jr. As his nickname, "Chicken Harry" suggests, Harry's business was chickens; his specialty was live-poultry. Nat Poland, a dealer on Front Street in Philadelphia, became a major customer. Victor's job was to haul chickens to Philadelphia late at night or in the early morning, then return home to prepare for the next trip. At that time, Harry H. Weaver Jr. was one of the few in the Lancaster area involved with the live-chicken business.[2]

FROM FATHER TO SON

Ralph Deckert of Ephrata bought the Sharon Hill Market building in suburban Philadelphia. He invited Victor's father, David H. Weaver, to open a stand in his farmers' market. A poster of that day advertised this enterprise as "The Lancaster County Farmers' Market House" opening to the public on May 18, 1935. The promotional poster emphasized the market's farm-fresh bounty from Lancaster County, the Garden Spot of America.

Victor's uncle, Harry H. Weaver Jr., nicknamed "Chicken Harry," was well known for his chicken business. Courtesy of Glenn Weaver.

Father and son probably shared conversations about this potential market for his poultry. Perhaps the Great Depression brought some lean years to the Weaver farm. Was their venture done on a whim with the hope of a little extra income, or was it a calculated decision to test the waters and future potential? In those times, necessity and opportunity blended together. For those with an entrepreneurial spirit, the future held promise. Another factor in the young couple's decision to consider this venture was father David's waning interest in attending his market stand. He discovered he didn't enjoy the market routine so he encouraged his son to take up the position.[3]

David found more fulfillment in the small feed warehouse business he began on his Weaverland farm. He sold and hauled feed locally. Garden seeds and some dressed poultry were among other offerings available at his warehouse. During the summer peach season,

---

· · ANNOUNCEMENT · ·

Opening of

LANCASTER COUNTY FARMERS
MARKET HOUSE

SATURDAY, MAY 18, 1935, 8 A. M.

In SHARON HILL, on Chester Pike at Clifton Ave.
ONE MILE SOUTH OF DARBY BUSINESS DISTRICT

THIS MARKET is composed of Lancaster County Farmers exclusively, with a complete line of reasonably priced fresh farm products from the *Garden Spot of America* such as: Fresh Meats, Smoked Meats, Lunch Meats, Fresh Killed Poultry, Butter, Eggs, Cheese, Preserves, Home-made Bread, Pastry, Egg Noodles, and all Vegetables and Fruit in their respective seasons.

ROUTES: Our Market House is located in Sharon Hill, on Chester Pike near Clifton Avenue, Route No. 13 between Philadelphia and Chester; one square from Philadelphia & West Chester Trolley Lines running between Sharon Hill and 69th Street, through Collingdale, Aldan, Lansdowne and Drexel Hill. Chester Pike Bus passes market every 15 minutes. Take Darby-Media Bus on MacDade Blvd., get off at Clifton Avenue, then walk 2 squares east to the market.

Market House will be open for business:

Every WEDNESDAY, 8 A. M. to 5 P. M.   Every SATURDAY 8 A. M. to 7 P. M.

Bring your market basket, you will need it when you see our line of Farm Products.
Don't miss Opening Day!   Tell your friends!   Ample Free Parking Space!

A Sharon Hill Market handbill advertisement of the Lancaster County Farmers' Market that began the market phase of Weaver Poultry. Courtesy of the Newswanger family.

David sold Adams County peaches to local people from the farm. The Weaver homestead became a busy center of activity as families arrived to claim their orders. Later, David left his farm business for New Holland where he became a representative of Eastern States Farmers' Exchange and later, Agway.

Victor's brother, Raymond H. Weaver, worked for Weaver during the initial years of the market phase, but he did not enjoy tending a market stand and the early morning trips to Philadelphia any more than his father had. He was happy to take over the home farm when his father moved on to other interests. There he found satisfaction as one of the successful farmers in the family. A unique feature of the farm was its location close to Ivan Martin's stone quarry. On blasting day, their windows rattled as the charges were set off.[4]

TO MARKET, TO MARKET

Leaving Lancaster County behind, Victor and Edith journeyed southward towards the suburbs of Philadelphia—this was indeed an adventure—what response would they get? That question was soon answered by their customers who bought their chickens. The young couple returned home greatly encouraged. Next week they would return. Now there were more questions to consider. How many chickens should they prepare? How many could they process in their kitchen? Did they have enough chickens on their farm to meet increasing demand? More questions came with each level of commitment to their operation.

Just a few months after starting with 17 chickens in 1937, over 200 broilers per week were being prepared for market. Some of the operation had to be moved to a tree outside the farmhouse. Bursting at the seams, the kitchen operation needed another home. The Weavers purchased a property on South Custer Avenue in New Holland, Pennsylvania, with potential to expand their operation. A shed on the new property became the next processing center for what was by now known as Weaver Poultry. Edith probably gave a sigh of relief at the prospect of reclaiming her kitchen![5]

The Weaver house is on the left. The large building referred to as "the shed" is in the background. Courtesy of the Newswanger family.

BENJAMIN L. BURKHOLDER

Benjamin L. Burkholder, the Weavers' first employee, joined the operation late in 1937. He remembers the shed on the Custer Avenue property as the first processing place in New Holland. He described it as an "old house, or dwelling of some sort, previously used as a machine shop and possibly even a place for drying tobacco." What renovations had to be made for its new function isn't known, but this became the first processing site for Weaver Poultry on the new property.[6]

Ben came to the Weavers without a résumé, but he already had market experience. His brother, Aaron Burkholder, was doing painting and paper hanging for the Weavers at Custer Avenue. When Victor asked Aaron if he knew anyone who might help them dress chickens, Aaron had a quick reply—his brother, Ben, was already helping out at home with their father's sideline market business.

The Burkholder family attended Windsor Market in Reading where they sold chickens, rabbits, noodles and garden produce. Ben's father, Andrew, began selling cut-up chicken at his market stand. This "created quite a stir." Other stand holders didn't appreciate this new trend and the extra work it involved. After school, young Ben dressed more than 20 rabbits for market and helped process chickens and ducks as well. He was an ideal prospect as an employee to join Weaver Poultry.[7]

Ben remembers Victor's fondness for Essex cars, which he drove faithfully until the Hudson Motor Company phased out the brand. After this, he was a loyal Hudson customer. In 1936, Hudson introduced the Terraplane model and Victor bought one. Ben later became the proud owner of the Terraplane. Victor sold the car to him for $150, and he "earned it off" over a period of time. Ben felt the car was a bit unusual, not a popular car, but his prized first car. He drove the Terraplane to Sharon Hill Market with a barrel of chickens in the trunk. By this time eggs, cheese and butter were part of the Weaver offerings. Ben stashed these things on the back seat. Fortunately there were no traffic accidents or scrambled eggs along the way, but the need for a truck became obvious.[8]

Victor's first pickup truck was a 1946 Hudson. He put a canvas cover over the truck bed when hauling products to Sharon Hill. Eventually they added a green International panel truck to help with their expanding market needs, which by then included Germantown. Victor's brother, Raymond, took Ben along in this truck to Germantown.

When another truck was purchased, it was also green, and
this set the forest green color
choice for many future trucks.

Ben Burkholder described
the Germantown customers as
"a very high class." Chauffeurs
in a procession of limousines
unloaded their passengers at
the front door and returned to
collect them at the end of their
shopping day. It was an interesting mix of cultures as Lancast-

Victor with his 1937 Hudson Terraplane. He soon passed it on to a young Ben Burkhold-er who had to "earn it off." Courtesy of the Newswanger family.

er County farmers met the "well-heeled" of Philadelphia. Due to the
strong demand for chicken during the wartime years, the company had
approximately 15 employees.

The Sharon Hill and Germantown Markets were located near
World War II defense plants. Many people with jobs there had money to spend. Unlike other meats, chicken was not rationed. This increased demand put additional pressure on farmers' supplies. Some
stand holders added inferior quality poultry to their showcases to
deepen their inventory. Weaver refused this temptation and continued
to offer a quality product, keeping their reputation intact.[9]

The war created a very different market atmosphere. Rationing of other meats and butter gave rise to a frantic buying mood.
Shoppers arriving at 5:30 in the morning formed a block-long line
waiting for the doors to open. When this finally happened, people
rushed to their favorite market stands, such as Weaver. In this atmosphere, selling chickens was easy. Customers, fearing their chicken
might be gone by their turn for service, reached over the countertops
to grab the desired chicken. Then they waited, chicken in hand, to
purchase their trophies. Stand holders could be sold out by 11:00 in
the morning.[10]

After the war, the end of food rationing brought a new dynamic to retail marketing. The long lines of waiting customers disappeared. Victor Weaver was quick to recognize this change. Customers no longer stood in line holding their anticipated purchases. Prompt, courteous service became the emphasis of the market stand. "Service to the customer" was the Weaver motto. As sales continued to increase, more help was needed to prepare chickens for market.[11]

As the company grew, Ben gained more responsibility and became a valuable asset for Victor. Ben was more of a risk-taker. He was ready to run with a project before all the details were worked out. Victor's perfectionism and desire to organize the details helped strike a balance. The two men made a good team. Another young man was about to join the growing number at Weaver and, like Ben, he grew with the company to become one of Victor's inner circle.

Ben Burkholder (center) with Melvin S. Mitchell, his right-hand man, on Ben's right, and an unidentified worker at Reading Terminal in Philadelphia. Courtesy of the New Holland Area Historical Society.

MELVIN S. MITCHELL

Ben Burkholder suggested they needed a young fellow to help catch chickens. It should be someone he could train to follow in his footsteps. Victor gave his approval, "so long as this fellow is ambitious and will sell like you and I do." That fellow was young Melvin Mitchell who turned out to be a good choice. Mitchell began his career at Weaver Poultry in 1945 when he was 14 years old.

He worked at Weaver after school and full time on Saturdays. "We did it all," he said. They candled eggs. They caught chickens, and were involved in every phase of preparing them for market. He attended market with Ben Burkholder at Sharon Hill.[12]

Mel quit high school after tenth grade. His family needed his help financially. He was a good worker who fit in well, and he progressed steadily upward within the company. Although he never earned his MBA, Mel availed himself of every opportunity to learn and took courses enabling him to do his job better. His innate abilities and continuing education were helpful to his advancement.

Melvin S. Mitchell joined Weaver after his sophomore year of high school. Courtesy of the New Holland Area Historical Society.

Mitchell identified two Dale Carnegie courses as foundational for him. One course was about human relations. The second course in sales seemed to fit him quite well. The Carnegie organization kept him on as an assistant instructor. During his three years in this role, he learned as much as he taught to others. Later Melvin became general manager of the Philadelphia suburban markets, and Ben Burkholder became wholesale manager of all markets. Weaver hired Mennonite city pastors to work in their Philadelphia stores as a way to support these urban churches.[13]

SHARON HILL MEMORIES

As a young teenager in the fifties, the author has memories of Sharon Hill Market. He attended the market with his uncle, Charles Gehman, who sold eggs from his small stand. He remembers the Weaver stand as a well-established, larger site back to back with the Gehman stand. Although he had little interchange with the people at Weaver's, the author was impressed with the size of their operation.

Market vendors in general were friendly people. During slow times, an employee of the produce stand across the aisle launched an occasional lima bean or other such rubber band-propelled missile at us.

The young man at the cut-up poultry stand next to Gehman's entertained the author with his meat cleaver dexterity. Brandishing his meat cleaver while rapidly moving his hand on and off the chopping block, he chopped away—always managing to miss his hand with every determined stroke.

Melvin Mitchell also remembers the skill of the meat cleaver men—in fact one day he lost part of his necktie to one of them! In their spare moments the young guys were always "clowning around," he said. The actual offender who took his necktie Mel thinks was possibly a David Landis. His meat stand was adjacent to Weaver's. There was a chopping block on the boundary between the two stands, maybe even shared by them. As Mel stood close by the chopping block watching a similar "hand-chopping" demonstration, Landis suddenly reached up, grabbed Mel's necktie, and with one stroke severed part of it from the startled owner! Mel chuckled as he related the story. "We worked hard, but we had fun too," he said. A little fun helped pass the time.[14]

One busy holiday season was especially demanding. Ben Burkholder decided to reward Mel, his younger prodigy, with a steak dinner on the way home. So they stopped at a restaurant and had a good dinner, but when it was time to pay the bill, Ben discovered he didn't have money for the tab. An earnest discussion followed with Ben suggesting that Mel pay up. Mel felt a promise had been made and refused to bail Ben out, saying it was "his problem." After a lengthy discussion, Mel relented and agreed to pay the bill as a loan. Apparently he had enough job security to enjoy Ben's discomfort in those circumstances, and he believes the loan was later paid. Even this experience was included in the "fun" of going to market.[15]

From its Sharon Hill opening in 1937, Weaver Poultry expanded into a dozen suburban Philadelphia markets and stores. The Kensington Market in 1959 was the last to open. Mitchell became general manager overseeing all these markets.

A CHANGE OF DIRECTION

After World War II, Weaver discovered future potential for sales could take their company in a new direction. The farmers' market era was declining. Consumers were attracted to the new self-service, grocery stores offering a great variety of products. The small, mom and pop corner grocery stores had difficulty competing with the one-stop shopping appeal of these new supermarkets. Weaver sold some of its market stands and stores to managers. Now everything had to be done on a grander scale to meet the demand of wholesale marketing with the continuing Weaver emphasis on a quality product. More variety of products would be needed for these new stores.

Weaver was already expanding with more processing facilities to meet demand. Egg operations moved to a building rented at the New Holland Sales Stables. Space at the New Holland Ice Plant provided needed storage for unsold products returned from market. A jellied chicken product and chicken scrapple became forerunners of later processed food products.

On May 29, 1946, Weaver Poultry reorganized as Victor F. Weaver, Inc. Corporate officers were as follows: Victor F. Weaver, president; Edith M. Weaver, secretary; and David H. Weaver, treasurer. After changes in the board of directors, Victor became president and treasurer; Edith, assistant treasurer; and B. Sylvan Horning, secretary. Boyd Wert, Lester Martin and Ben Burkholder completed the executive committee. This act of incorporation reflected the company's continued growth and organization for the future. Incorporation increased the perception of Weaver's credibility and legitimacy as a business and provided more protection for corporate risk-taking necessary for growth.[16]

The new plant at Weaver was completed in 1946. It would be an important asset in the changing nature of sales and the volume of production the fifties demanded. While at one time Weaver believed processing 30 chickens per minute would be the maximum necessary, the company was continually challenged to boost production capacities upward in numbers difficult to envision just a few years before. New chicken products were also a challenge.

Victor and Edith Weaver used their kitchen to experiment with a new prepared food product. Packaged as Weaver Fried Chicken, it was pre-cooked, battered, breaded and fried. For consumers in 1946,

The Weaver plant in the 1950s. Janet was born in the white house by the main plant entrance. It became the Burkholder's house, in 1950, when the Weavers built their new house just beyond it. Janet lived there until she married in 1962. The New Holland Sales Stables owned the field beyond the Weavers' property. Zausner's Cheese plant now occupies the upper left corner of that property. Courtesy of the Newswanger family.

prepared foods were a departure from the traditional fresh chicken offerings. The product, initially well received, declined in sales with the
increased abundance of fresh chicken after the war. Weaver was ahead
of the times with this idea. It would be revived later with much greater
success.[17]

When Victor and Edith Weaver began their adventure into the
world of retail sales, they were testing the waters for the future. What
began as a small family business with only a couple of employees,
would soon show signs of vitality and growth. They developed personal relationships with many customers. These face-to-face connections not only sold the product, but also affirmed the integrity of
those behind the counter. From the beginning, quality of product and
the relationship with customers emerged as the fundamental business
philosophy of the Weavers.

CHAPTER 3

Philhaven Hospital:
A Life-long Service Commitment

STIRRINGS OF MENTAL HEALTH REFORM

Victor Weaver's successful business was only part of his story. His involvement in many causes outside the business world also provided some insights about him. His association with Philhaven Hospital, established for treatment of the mentally ill, was one of his most enduring commitments of community service.

Philhaven Hospital began in 1948. The daily charge for patient care was $6.25. Courtesy of Betty Greider.

In the 1840s Dorothea Dix roused the nation's consciousness with demands for change in the treatment of mentally ill citizens. Instead of treatment, there was incarceration and isolation. She found many living in chains as part of local jails' brutal conditions. The treatment of those in poorhouses wasn't any better. Dix resolved to remove these people from their difficult situations and to create a more healthy environment for their benefit as a positive first step. Dix's work was foundational in creating the first system of asylums in the nation.

State-run hospitals, or asylums, functioned as self-sustaining communities. Patients got humane treatment, lived, and worked there. On hospital farms, they helped raise the institution's food. For many, work was a welcome alternative to a vegetative existence. These asylums were intended to be places of safety. Patients were out of the mainstream of a society that had little empathy or understanding of them—it was a major step away from that difficult past.

But over time the system developed problems. Isolated from public awareness, these places of refuge had become more custodial than therapeutic in the years between 1890-1940—more like jails than places of hope. The term "asylum" took on a new and troubling meaning.[1]

World War II added to the difficulties of state hospitals in several ways. When administrative staff left their employment for better paying jobs in defense industries, and other staff members were drafted, many were not replaced. Hospital populations rose at alarming rates while staff numbers declined. For example, in 1941, Byberry, the Philadelphia State Hospital, had a patient population of 3,500 and staff of 1,000. A year later, 200 staff were responsible for 6,100 patients![2]

Although war brought more pressures to the asylum system, it also set in motion forces that ultimately revitalized treatment of the mentally ill. Americans were beginning to examine the stigma attached to mental illness with a growing realization that beyond the traumas of war, there were other issues of mental illness in society that needed to be addressed.

During World War I, soldiers returning from combat with severe psychological symptoms were described as "shell shocked." Some military leaders considered them to be "malingering and cowardly."

As the United States mobilized for World War II, psychologists attempted to screen out inductees who might be susceptible to shell shock. By 1943, it was evident that their efforts were failing. "War neurosis" was the new diagnosis for over a million troops admitted to US hospitals. In 1944, admissions were as high as 250 per thousand in combat units. By the end of the war, veterans qualified for disability benefits under a diagnosis of "psychoneurosis."

Conditions of public and Veterans Hospitals, ignored by states for decades, now came under federal scrutiny and the attention of journalists. In the July 1946 *Reader's Digest*, Albert Deutsch charged that the "quality of care had regressed to that of the asylums of the nineteenth century serving to only provide custody rather than care of the mentally sick."[3]

CIVILIAN PUBLIC SERVICE WORKERS' HOSPITAL EXPERIENCES

The Civilian Public Service (CPS) program administered by Selective Service during World War II, made it possible for conscientious objectors to perform "work of national importance" for government agencies as an alternative to military service. The Peace Church denominations were responsible for the multimillion dollar yearly budget for the CPS program. The Weavers contributed several thousand dollars to the fund.

While many worked in assignments for the Fish and Wildlife Service, Forest Service, or the National Park Service, some believed they could contribute more significant service in the nation's mental hospitals. When given permission to serve there, they were disturbed by what they saw.[4]

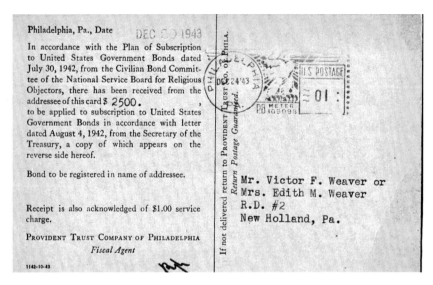

Philadelphia, Pa., Date   DEC 2 0 1943

In accordance with the Plan of Subscription to United States Government Bonds dated July 30, 1942, from the Civilian Bond Committee of the National Service Board for Religious Objectors, there has been received from the addressee of this card $ 2500. , to be applied to subscription to United States Government Bonds in accordance with letter dated August 4, 1942, from the Secretary of the Treasury, a copy of which appears on the reverse side hereof.

Bond to be registered in name of addressee.

Receipt is also acknowledged of $1.00 service charge.

PROVIDENT TRUST COMPANY OF PHILADELPHIA
Fiscal Agent

1142-10-43

If not delivered return to PROVIDENT TRUST CO. OF PHILA. *Return Postage Guaranteed.*

Mr. Victor F. Weaver or
Mrs. Edith M. Weaver
R.D. #2
New Holland, Pa.

Victor and Edith supported the Civilian Public Service program. The traditional Peace Churches partnered with the government to meet the program's costs. Courtesy of the Newswanger family.

The understaffed and overcrowded conditions in these hospitals quickly initiated them into the realities of asylum life. Staff members overwhelmed by the sheer number of patients feared losing control. Some feared for their personal safety. One response was to maintain control with an us-versus-them mentality of authority. This solution was especially true with regard to patients who didn't respond to electro or insulin shock treatments. Patients on these wards were the most difficult to control and conditions there were most shocking.

CPS worker, David Yoder, remembers a patient at Greystone Hospital. The man's deformed body and clenched fists reflected his mental anguish and neglect. Yoder began to give his personal attention to this man, washing his clenched hands and arms. Other CPS workers responded to what they saw with hands-on love. It was a concrete beginning of a growing belief that there had to be a better way to minister to the mentally ill.

What could such a small group of workers accomplish in light of such overwhelming numbers? The American Friends Service Committee unit at Byberry Hospital in Philadelphia got permission from superintendent Dr. Charles A. Zeller to collect stories of their experiences. Other hospital units contributed their stories as well. While compiling these accounts, Harold Barton and Willard Hetzel experienced their emotional impact. Overwhelmed, they found it difficult to continue their work. Selective Service officials agreed to relieve these men of their ward duties making this work less stressful. One result of this work was the Mental Hygiene Program of CPS. It was the forerunner of the National Mental Health Foundation.

Believing that the public needed to be informed, The American Friends Service Committee decided to publish their findings. The May 6, 1946, *Life Magazine* issue ran Albert Q. Maisel's article about the desperate state of mental health care complete with pictures of life on the wards. *Reader's Digest* also ran a condensed story of the article. These stories reverberated throughout the nation.[5]

The title of Albert Maisel's *Life Magazine* article, "Bedlam: Most U.S. Mental Hospitals Are a Shame and a Disgrace," set the tone. He contended these institutions were "doing little for the care and cure of the mentally ill." In fact, he believed they were "little more than the concentration camps of the [Bergen]-Belsen pattern." These were strong words for Americans still shocked by the emerging details of the Nazi death camps of World War II.

Maisel described the severely overcrowded wards and patients sleeping on the floor. Many didn't have clothing to wear. Restraints used to control patients might be used for months at a time. Sometimes patients died as a result of staff disciplinary actions. Cause of death in such situations seldom became public knowledge.

Attendants administered drugs on the wards without proper medical supervision. Buildings, in a state of disrepair, lacked such basics as water and showers. One governor said he believed the cows on his state's institutional farms got better care![6]

In his article, Maisel recognized the role of CPS workers and the documented evidence they presented. Although there were attempts to discredit this story, the amount of evidence overwhelmed all attempts of denial. His article also included the work of Walter Lerch, a *Cleveland Press* reporter. In October 1943, Lerch ran a front-page story in the *Press* including recognition of CPS documentation at the Cleveland State Hospital.

Ohio Governor, John Bricker, appointed Dr. Frank Tallman to fill the long-vacant position as State Commissioner of Mental Hygiene. After investigation, the commission's scathing report added weight to Tallman and Lerch's advocacy. The Ohio legislature appropriated $17,000,000 to begin building new hospital facilities. With Tallman's oversight at Cleveland, many of the abominable practices of the past were abandoned. Emphasis on care and cure replaced the desperate custodial patient warehousing of the past.[7]

FINDING A BETTER WAY

When CPS workers returned home, they took their experiences and concerns with them in their hearts. They continued to express their belief that a better way had to be found to treat the mentally ill. They refused to let the issue rest. Mennonite Church leaders, sympathetic to their concerns, pondered the issue. Was there a role for the church to play? Could the church help to find that better way?

In January 1944, Lancaster and Franconia Mennonite Conference leaders met with Amish bishops for a time of discussion. After several hours, two proposals surfaced. First, they affirmed the need for an "institution for the mentally sick." Second, they would consider a specific property some believed to be an ideal location for the hospital. Later, after exploration, the intended property appeared too elaborate for the beginning of such a work. Although the location of a facility wasn't clear, commitment to this new mission for the church continued to evolve.

A Hospital Study Committee of three men, Simon G. Bucher, Bishop J. Paul Graybill, and Noah W. Risser, agreed to study the question of a facility location. Although the facility issue remained unclear, commitment to this ministry deepened. Elvin G. Lefever, who became hospital administrator, described J. Paul Graybill as "one who was pushing this mission commitment pretty much." It's possible that his own struggles with depression—commonly referred to as "nerve problems" in those days—added to his intensity of advocacy. In time the location of such a facility became clear. Philhaven Hospital, located near Mt. Gretna, Pennsylvania, became that reality.[8]

Bishop J. Paul Graybill was a staunch advocate of the role he believed the church could play in mental health reform. Courtesy of Roy S. Burkholder.

Even after Philhaven's founding, CPS workers continued to advocate for the mentally ill. Two of them spoke of their convictions at the annual meeting of the Lancaster Mennonite Hospital Conference meeting held at Rohrerstown Mennonite Church. Some of the topics for discussion indicated developing church thinking. It was a time of education and increased sensitivity regarding mental illness.

Titus Brooks spoke on the topic, "The Need for a Mental Health Program in Church and Community." According to Brooks, "it would be unchristian" to overlook the mentally ill. He stressed that a sympathetic attitude made a difference in a Christian hospital. Harry Swarr's topic, "Can It Be Done?," was still an honest question in the minds of some. Arthur Kraybill and John Winters presented "Observations and Experiences in a Mental Hospital During CPS." Kraybill believed Jesus would show loving concern for such patients. The church should do the same. John Winters asked who would care for the "feebleminded and incurables" if not done by the church? He believed the Christian approach and the love of a faith community were an important part such a ministry.[9]

A CHARTER BOARD MEMBER

When Philhaven Hospital opened its doors offering psychiatric care in 1948, Victor Weaver was one of the 12 charter board members. He served that institution for almost 40 years—more than half his lifetime. Victor put aside the cares of his business to faithfully attend board meetings at Philhaven. Sometimes the trip there was the most exciting part of the day as illustrated by this well-known story.

Abram Horst Sr., a successful New Holland, Pennsylvania, building contractor, and Victor were traveling together to Philhaven. Abe was driving. He was rumored to be in a hurry when on the road, this day even more so. They were late. Somewhere along the way, their speeding car caught a policeman's attention, and he gave chase. His flashing lights soon flagged them to a stop. The officer approached their car and inquired what could possibly have been the reason for such haste. Supposedly Abe simply stated, with authority while gesturing towards Victor, "I'm taking this man to Philhaven!" "Follow me!" the officer said as he returned to his cruiser, and with lights flashing, escorted the men on this "emergency" mission. So instead of a speeding ticket, he gave Philhaven an endorsement! The point of the story, regardless of the likely embellishments, was that Philhaven had become a recognized part of this community's new era of psychiatric care. How Victor responded to this bold move by Abe isn't known.

All of the board's members belonged to the Lancaster Mennonite Conference, but similarities ended there. Some were businessmen, farmers, churchmen, and teachers who didn't know each other well but began to work together in their new roles.

The following story is one indication they were beginning to know each other better: Prior to the convening of a board meeting, Victor engaged Elvin G. Kreider sitting next to him in a conversation that went something like this: Victor, "So you hunt deer?" Elvin confirmed this, and with feeling Victor responded, "I don't think I could kill a deer!" "Well, Victor," the hunter replied, "think of all those chickens you kill every day!" "Oh," Victor replied, "I never thought of it that way!" Hopefully the call to order ended the awkward moment.[10]

Why was Victor so dedicated to the Philhaven cause he served for so many years? Victor's daughter, Janet, said in those days if the church asked you to serve in a particular position, you did it. Perhaps once committed to a task, he continued with a sense of duty and belief in the mental health mission. A former employee answered the question this way, "Victor was a very caring person regarding people in general and persons with disabilities in particular."

Another significant influence was likely when he became aware of an employee's struggle with mental illness, and how it affected their life and work. The following story illustrates Victor's personal involvement with such an employee and his family. A family member relates the following story:

> When I was a junior at Upper Leacock High School, my father was in the middle of a mental health crisis. My three brothers had married and left home. My sister was in nursing school in Lancaster. The full burden of assisting my mother in this crisis fell on my shoulders. The doctor ordered me to follow my dad whenever he went out to our little barn. I was to watch him intently to make sure he did not harm himself.

> One day I came home to an empty house. Things had collapsed at work. Victor Weaver drove my father and mom to Philhaven. My dad was admitted for mental health care. Victor was an officer on the board at Philhaven and probably used his influence to get dad immediate treatment.

> Dad was still working at Weaver's a few years later after several periods of treatment at Philhaven. Times at work were challenging. The push for profits was squeezed by business competition. Farmers were

looking for the highest dollar for their egg sales. Weaver management wanted to cut prices, but dad was an advocate for the farmers' interests. During this time, there was sharp disagreement. Later, Victor spoke with my dad about this time. He said he was sorry for the stressful situation dad had been in. He promised dad a job at Weaver as long as he needed one. Victor's compassion moved my father deeply.[11]

A RELUCTANT PUBLIC SPEAKER'S GROWING INVOLVEMENT

At annual meetings of the Lancaster Mennonite Hospital Association, board members continued to address CPS workers' concerns and to educate their fellow members. Victor Weaver's daughter, Janet, remembers his baptism of fire as he confronted his aversion to public speaking. A somewhat shy and retiring person, Victor wouldn't volunteer for such a duty, but each board member had to prepare a three-minute speech on an assigned topic. Even more distressing, this speech wasn't relegated to the familiar confines of a board meeting, but his audience would be the assembly at Mellinger Mennonite Church for the annual meeting of the Lancaster Mennonite Hospital Association. Victor's topic—"The Care of Mental Patients"—needed careful thought and preparation. This experience drew him beyond his comfort zone, and the "fat was now in the fire," so to speak. He didn't shrink from this new responsibility.[12]

He resolved to address his situation with technology. After purchasing a wire recorder, the best of that day, he diligently practiced giving his speech at home. It was a painful process, but he kept at it, determined to succeed in this unpleasant assignment.

One result of Victor's long involvement with Philhaven was that he grew personally along with his responsibilities. At the beginning, he was a reluctant public speaker, but hospital board minutes reveal him serving in a variety of assignments over the years. In 1963, Victor gave the board the report of the Building and Grounds Committee regarding completed paving and landscaping around the new chapel. Other reports of his involvement are sprinkled throughout board minutes. In 1965, Victor joined the Personnel Committee as an additional duty. A few years later, he served on the Study Committee formed to assess the future hospital facilities needs and program.

The March 12, 1970, minutes note Vice Chairman Victor convened the board meeting due to Noah Kreider's absence. Victor became board chair at the June 10, 1971, meeting. Fellow New Holland businessman, Abram Horst, was elected vice chairman. Perhaps it was during this time when they traveled together that they enjoyed the alleged police escort to Philhaven.

Chairman Weaver began his leadership with a difficult issue. The minutes described a "deadlock" between the Medical Staff and the Administration. Attorney Elvin B. Byler was also on hand for this difficult meeting. It isn't clear if Byler was there as a mediator or to represent the doctor involved. So Victor got his baptism of fire presiding at this first meeting.[13]

One of Victor's behind-the-scenes actions had great significance for the development of Philhaven. When Elvin G. Lefever spoke of leaving his administrative post, the search was on for a successor. A young man in the Weaverland Mennonite congregation caught Victor's attention. He knew Horace Martin and his family well. As he became aware of Horace's interest in a nursing career, Victor conferred with Bishop J. Paul Graybill. Convinced Horace was a possible candidate for the Philhaven position, the two men followed his progress.

Martin's Civilian Public Service assignment gave him experiences in psychiatric nursing care at the Howard State Hospital of Rhode Island. He also became familiar with the work and concerns of CPS workers at the hospital. These experiences helped shape his nursing career focus.

After discharge from his service assignment, Horace worked to complete his high school degree. That done, he enrolled at the Pennsylvania Hospital School of Nursing for Men.

Horace and Arlene Martin made their home at Philhaven and took up the task of leadership after Horace graduated from nurses' training. Courtesy of Miriam Martin Frey.

When nearly finished with his studies there, Horace had an unusual job offer. His wife, Arlene, received the phone call at their apartment. Bishop John Martin was calling regarding a position at Philhaven. When Arlene inquired what shift was being offered, the bishop's reply surprised her—Philhaven wanted Horace to consider becoming their administrator!

The young couple visited Philhaven to evaluate this imposing assignment. The decision made to accept the job, the Martins took up residence on campus. Horace Martin was 28 years old when he became Philhaven's administrator, he served in this role for the next 18 years.[14]

Victor Weaver's long tenure on the hospital board, along with other members, gave the young Horace the stabilizing support he needed as he took up this work. Victor was content to keep a low profile in board meetings. A colleague who served with Victor on another board provided some insight into how he conducted himself in those board meetings. He likely functioned in a similar fashion on the Philhaven Hospital board.

The colleague observed Victor as one of the quietest listeners in the room. He was a very humble man who sat and listened to others and appeared to be more interested in their thoughts than interjecting his own. He didn't flaunt his business success, and one would never guess that he was the successful businessman of a large corporation. When asked for his opinions, his insightful comments revealed the depth of his thinking. His opinions were well formed and had a depth that spoke of a good self-esteem. For Victor, the still waters did indeed run deep.[15]

Victor's commitment to service at Philhaven likely increased as he saw the unfolding significance of its mission, finding another way to treat mental illness. But there was an even more personal reason for his long term of service. Family members agreed that Philhaven's board became Victor's "church." Although he was committed to his home congregation, he found a special community among his peers on the board. Here he found associates who listened to his questions and the issues he faced as a business person. With no disrespect intended, this group's counsel became more meaningful to him than his bishop's efforts.

It is interesting to note that son, Dale, found a similar bond of community with his involvement in the Mennonite Economic Development Associates' work. Founded in 1953, these Mennonite entrepreneurs shared their experience to promote small and medium business solutions to poverty in many parts of the world.[16]

In 1984, lone charter board member, Victor F. Weaver, and Board President, Roy L. Bomberger, broke ground for The Continuing Challenge expansion project. Courtesy of WellSpan Philhaven.

After his term as board president, Victor continued to serve on the board as the only remaining charter member. In 1987, after more than 39 years of service, failing health forced Victor's resignation. He remained a loyal financial supporter even after his death a few years later.

In 2020, WellSpan Philhaven honored Victor and Edith Weaver with the establishment of the Legacy Circle. The hospital recognized Victor for his leadership of the ambitious building program that expanded Philhaven facilities, and Edith's initiation of the ministry to knit blankets for patients. A major trust fund gift to WellSpan Philhaven continues the couple's support of mental health programs, and the Weaver's United Service Foundation provides funding for a multi-year project to strengthen marriage and families.

WellSpan Philhaven's Legacy Circle program established in honor of Victor and Edith Weaver invites others to share the vision with their financial support. Courtesy of WellSpan Philhaven.

CHAPTER 4

Changing Direction: The Wholesale Market, 1950-1960s

SUPERMARKETS AND SUPER SALES

In the 1950s, times were changing. The opening of supermarkets brought a new energy and direction to food merchandising. Small corner grocery stores and farmers' markets faded in comparison to these new stores. Shoppers found these self-service, one-stop shopping establishments attractive.

Convenience and price superseded personal interaction between proprietor and customer. Despite such changes, Weaver continued to emphasize service and the quality of their products. Assessing consumer appetites, or creating them with new offerings, became an important way to stay ahead of competition. Weaver recognized the potential for selling their chicken wholesale to satisfy the growing demand of these superstores. As the company began to move in that direction, a new member was added to the team.[1]

William Pellman joined Weaver in 1950 to develop their wholesale markets. He didn't come with any sales experience that made him an attractive candidate for the job, but Victor had the ability to assess a prospective employee's character and potential. For him, education was less important than character and abilities. Bill said, "Victor looked at you, assessed your potential, and took a chance.

He gave you room to run." So Pellman took on the responsibility for developing Weaver wholesale accounts with his own game plan. He believed Victor had confidence in his ability to handle the assignment and didn't second-guess decisions.[2]

The Food Fair grocery chain gave Bill his first high volume account. Others soon followed including Armour, Swift, Wilson, Acme, Penn Food and A&P. Big orders for Weaver brought new challenges to meet this demand with more employees and new equipment.

Bill Pellman began adding supermarkets' wholesale accounts that bolstered Weaver's change of direction. Courtesy of New Holland Area Historical Society.

In 1956, another Weaver wholesale market innovation was cut-up poultry. When chickens suffered bruises in processing, they could not be sold as whole chickens. Cut up to eliminate these bruised parts and sold as grade "A" chicken, they became popular with consumers to the point that even perfect chickens had to be cut up to meet the demand. It was a welcome solution to the problem.[3]

That same year, Weaver added refrigerated tractor-trailer trucks to its fleet to serve supermarkets. By 1979, one of their drivers, Lee Weaver, reached

Lee Weaver became the first Weaver truck driver to log one million accident-free miles. Courtesy of New Holland Area Historical Society.

the one-million-mile marker without a preventable accident or major traffic citation. Although citizens' band radios were quite popular by this time, Lee didn't have one because he believed they were more of a distraction to safe driving than a necessity. Although he was never involved in an accident, Lee experienced some close calls on the road. His focus on caution and courtesy helped him avoid some accidents despite motorists' impatience, speed, and lack of control in some situations. He summed up his success saying, "I did my best and left the rest up to God."

A fundamental rule for Weaver truck drivers was to honor Sunday as a day of rest by not leaving the yard until 12:01 Monday morning. When questioned whether truckers eager to get on the road were fudging this prohibition, he was doubtful, saying in his experience, it was a well-kept admonition. The Burkholder family lived on the plant site in the Weavers' first house. Some have said that Ben may have brought early exits to a halt encouraging truckers to wait just a few more minutes for Monday morning's official sendoff.[4]

Larry Newswanger remembers hearing the truck engines starting. It was an indication he would soon have to end his date with the Weavers' daughter, Janet, and be on the road to meet his curfew at home.

Weaver's tractor trailer fleet's graphics earned it an honorable mention in 1982 for its fleet markings and color schemes promoting safety. Such markings are intended to help make a truck noticeable even during the daytime. Beyond the safety issue, Mel Mitchell explained the forward-slanting parallelogram signified a forward-mov-

Weaver trucks won an honorable mention for graphic design promoting safety. The forward slanting Weaver parallelogram is to suggest the progressive nature of the company. Courtesy of New Holland Area Historical Society.

ing company while the style of the Weaver name is reminiscent of the company's early years. The slogan on the trailers' sides, "Helping to feed your family better!," personalized the company's desire to deliver a quality product to the nation's dinner tables. Painted white, the trailers were to symbolize the sanitary conditions of Weaver processing its quality products.[5]

With the beginning of a personnel department, John Kennel took over the responsibility for hiring employees. His role was also vital in cultivating positive employee relationships necessary for production to flow smoothly. Unlike many earlier employees who were part of the management team, John had a college education. When a prospective job interviewee told John he had a college degree, John, tongue in cheek, assured the applicant that this wouldn't be held against him! He got the job.

NEW PRODUCTS, A NEW DIRECTION

In 1959, the federal government initiated a poultry inspection law. Prior to this, Weaver worked voluntarily with state inspectors, but now compliance with federal laws brought noteworthy changes.

According to federal standards if blisters on chicken breasts had to be trimmed, the chicken could no longer be sold as grade "A" quality. In 1960, Dale M. Weaver, Executive Vice President, gave leadership to a new products development team. The team produced a processed chicken steak utilizing these trimmed breasts. Local restaurants and stores served as a test market. While the steaks had some appeal, the results didn't indicate great market potential.

The next initiative was to use chicken breasts in an emulsified product. Equipment used to make chicken scrapple in the early market days was repurposed for this endeavor. The product was pasteurized and packaged in a casing Union Carbide developed. Introduced as the Weaver Chicken Roll, it soon became a deli hit.

In 1959 Weaver's Quality Eggs, Inc. became a separate department of the company. As a boy, Lamar Weaver remembers that Sunday dinners at the Weaver home often included a leisurely walk looking around the plant. As a young man, Lamar worked for his father, Raymond, on the family farm. During slack times on the farm and later, during his college years, he looked to his Uncle Victor for work. Lamar found work in the Egg and Maintenance Departments.

Working evenings in the Egg Department, he soon learned about Ben Burkholder's evening strolls through the facility. Ben and his family lived next door to Victor and Edith on the South Custer Avenue site. Part of his responsibility was overall plant supervision. Some nights when he had trouble sleeping, Ben's evening strolls included a visit to the Egg Department. On such occasions, word spread quickly among workers—"Big Ben is in the building!" While all was usually in order, it was especially important on these occasions to be at work, as expected, busily candling eggs with no evidence of horseplay or other tomfoolery. Ben was a tall, physically imposing figure and also recognized by the workers for his high position within the company. He knew Lamar's father well and that Victor was Lamar's uncle. Lamar didn't want any unfavorable reports filtering back to either one.[6]

Work at the Egg Department went on day and night. Courtesy of New Holland Area Historical Society.

THE BROILER FARMERS' SUPPLY LINE

As Weaver Poultry grew from its elementary beginnings at Sharon Hill Market, the growing demand for chicken made apparent the need for a steady flow of birds for daily processing. That demand soon expanded beyond the Weavers' Blue Ball farm to neighboring farms. Eventually a network of Weaver Broiler Growers located within a 25-mile radius of Weaver supplied the daily needs of the New Holland plant. Prior to this arrangement however, broiler growers from as far away as Delaware were part of that supply chain. While the following incident in itself did not cause this change, it illustrated the vulnerability of an extended supply line.

In the 1950s, Weaver got some of its poultry from Delaware through a broker at the Delaware Chicken Exchange. The broker's brother had the responsibility, as weight master, to supervise the catching crews and get the trucks on their way to the Weaver plant in New Holland. While this arrangement functioned well most of the time, on one particular night, things didn't go well. Three trucks needed to be loaded for the trip to New Holland.

Heavy rain and a muddy lane made access to the chicken house especially difficult. In the process of positioning the last trailer, it had to be disengaged from the tractor. When the tractor was hooked up again, it wasn't apparent that the hitch was not fully engaged until the truck began to pull away. Only then, as the trailer slipped from the tractor and fell to the ground with a sickening thud, did the workers realize their error. Too heavy to be raised, the trailer load of chicken crates had to be unloaded, the trailer jacked up and re-hitched to the tractor, crates reloaded, and then finally it was on its way north. The time-consuming processes had repercussions at the other end of the line in New Holland where the expected arrival didn't occur and the waiting plant had to shut down.

A few weeks later, Victor made a trip to Delaware to see what had happened and was not very happy about the incident and the vulnerability it posed for the future. As the broiler growing program developed closer to home base, the Delaware exchange declined significantly due to Weaver's disengagement.[7]

Weaver developed their broiler system in league with independent farmer-growers providing the facilities and daily care of their young flocks. Weaver servicemen monitored and inspected these flocks in over 120 modern environmentally-controlled broiler houses producing 26 million broilers each year for the New Holland plant. Another 17 million were raised by broiler growers in the Gainesville, Georgia, area and processed at the Gainesville plant.

The whole process began with breeder stock in Fayetteville, North Carolina, and in Lancaster County, Pennsylvania. These two facilities provided the eggs to be hatched. The Longenecker-Weaver hatchery in Elizabethtown was responsible for the incubation. The chicks were distributed to more than 50 broiler growers in Central and Eastern Pennsylvania.

Weaver's purchase of the North Carolina breeder's company proved to be a wise move. Weaver merged the breeder company with a small feed business, and the two became Central Farms, Inc. The arrangement worked well for Weaver.

Due to its remote location in North Carolina, the company's breeder stock had little threat from disease. This was a major advantage in comparison to the Lancaster unit. Ben Burkholder and Allon Lefever's management there for ten years prior to the addition of the Boaz plant helped them to understand labor relations in the southern culture. It was good preparation for making the Boaz plant a successful operation.

Since male chicks matured more quickly than pullets, chicks were separated by sex and given the special feed appropriate for each. The goal was to have both pullets and cockerels close to a uniform size at maturity. Planners were looking ahead to packaging chicken breasts in 22-ounce boxes at the end of the processing line. If the actual weight was under 22 ounces, the company could be in trouble with government regulations; if the weight was several ounces over, the company was losing money.

From hatchery to mature bird, raising broilers became a precise science with the goal of a consistent quality product. Another example of Weaver's progressive style of operations was having Dr. Singletary, a veterinarian, on its staff. Another aspect of Weaver's science was genetic research to select the desired traits of fast-growing, healthy chicken with tender, choice meat characteristics. All phases of the development were carefully monitored to promote a healthy growth cycle. Assessment of efficient feed conversion to weight gain, and regular flock inspections by the company veterinarian nurtured the birds to maturity within 6 or 7 weeks.[8]

In 1963, Paul G. Brubaker and wife Martha, became the fifth farmer of Weaver Broiler Growers in a venture that would ultimately become a tradition including his four sons and their families. When Paul heard about the Weaver program, he was looking for an alternative to raising tobacco, a crop that "did little to improve the food situation and bothered him." If he quit raising tobacco, he needed income to supplement his dairy herd.

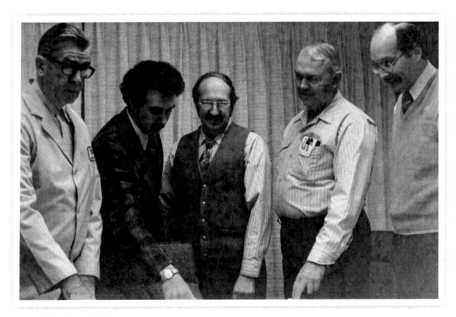

Dr. Singletary, company veterinarian, watched over development of the Weaver Broiler Farmers' stock. Having a veterinarian on staff was another example of Weaver progressivism. Courtesy of New Holland Area Historical Society.

Paul's two broiler houses built in 1963 together cost $70,000. Since then, there have been many upgrades in broiler housing construction for added energy efficiency and flock management. "Chicken talk" was a staple of conversation at Brubaker family gatherings. Odd-man-out at family gatherings, teacher Dale had his four brothers' sympathy, but talking business was irresistible among these men with 14 broiler houses.

Having more time to spend with their young families was an attractive benefit for the Brubakers. Dairy herds were phased out of several farming operations as time demands grew. The broiler schedule gave these families a flexibility not possible for dairy farmers. For example, John and Sharon Brubaker posted their son's athletic schedule right alongside their broiler calendar. They were free to attend their children's activities.

Avid hunters, John and Robert, could rely on their wives during hunting season to keep things going at home. John's wife, Sharon, noted that during such times, "More often than not, there were either young chicks or birds almost ready to go." Robert's wife, Lois, enjoyed daily tending their flocks freeing him to oversee other aspects of the farming operation. When possible, the families staggered vacations so that at least one of the brothers was at home to deal with emergency situations. Having their farms close to each other was an added convenience in these situations.

Paul Brubaker Sr. summed up the family's relationship to Weaver as a positive experience. Early in his broiler days, a competitor suggested he join their company, but he declined. The high moral and business principles of the Weaver company kept him loyal to his commitments. "They always tried to follow Christian ideals," he said.

Today the fourth generation of Brubakers continues the broiler farming tradition Paul and Martha began in 1963. Son Robert Brubaker Sr. and wife, Lois, have two sons, Robert Jr. and Randy. Both have been broiler farmers with years of experience that they are now passing on to their sons. Robert Jr.'s sons, Hunter and Nick, have started their

Robert Brubaker Sr. and wife Lois, stand with some members of the Brubaker family in front of present-day broiler houses. From left to right: Hunter, Bob Jr., Bob Sr., Lois, Randy, Graham, Max, Ella, Jodie, Ava Brubaker.

own farms. Randy's son, Max, is planning to build broiler houses on his recently purchased farm. Robert Sr. described the decision to become a broiler farmer as "life changing," impacting generations beyond anything he dreamed of when he decided to continue his father's work.

The Brubakers are proud of their farming tradition and, Lois wrote, "glad for Victor Weaver's foresight that we could carry out this occupation for four generations." They saw Victor as "a businessman with ethical values, wisdom and the ability to choose the right people for the right job." One of those people was Jacob Musser who was the grow-out manager for Weaver. Jake supervised the servicemen who made weekly farm visits to care for the flocks' development.[9]

UNIONS AND THE TREATMENT OF EMPLOYEES

In the fifties, the goal of the labor movement was to continue expanding union membership, and increasing benefits through collective bargaining or strikes.

The family atmosphere at Weaver included people relating on a first-name basis at all levels in the company. The ability to communicate across cultures was important for many reasons. Victor wanted to be open and fair in dealing with employees so that third-party intervention, such as a union, wouldn't be necessary. His believed issues of dissatisfaction could be more effectively addressed within the company based on the personal relationships fostered over time. His own model of caring and individual attention to people at any level was a good example of his sincerity and Christian ideals rather than a strategy of control.

Victor feared that in any direct meeting with union organizers, the company's words could be misconstrued in the newspapers giving Weaver bad press. When it came to using words, or putting thoughts on paper, Victor relied on Ben Burkholder and others for such situations; figures were his forte, not words. There was other help for Victor from his church.[10]

On June 6, 1941, Mennonite and Brethren in Christ Churches released a position statement on industrial relations. It advocated an "emphasis on the principle of love and nonresistance opposed to retaliation in all human relations and a spirit of good will manifest to all." It discouraged Christian employers' use of "coercive methods," as not being in harmony with their faith and exhorted them to treat workers justly, "removing every occasion for grievances, strife or conflict."

In December 1952, the Committee on Economic and Social Relations of the Mennonite Church held a meeting in Goshen, Indiana. Mennonite employers were invited to hear those trained in employer-employee relations present ways for Christian employers to better meet conditions in industry.

A similar meeting was planned for October 31, 1953, at East Chestnut Street Mennonite Church in Lancaster, Pennsylvania. Clarence E. Lutz, Secretary of the Lancaster Mennonite Conference Committee on Industrial Relations, sent a letter to invite, "A small, select group of employers and leaders of industry [who] would gather to discuss ways and means of maintaining better employer-employee relations." Victor was invited to join this group.

CAMP HEBRON

Victor enjoyed Camp Hebron as a place where he could relax from the pressures of business beyond the fishbowl at home on South Custer Avenue. As the expanding Weaver plant grew around the Weaver home, any activity was observable to employees and others driving by. Camp Hebron became a place of respite for the family. They enjoyed sharing this peaceful natural setting with others. The extended Weaver family sometimes shared Victor's and their parents' cabins for times together.

When the Weavers' neighbors built an addition to their cabin, Victor eagerly joined helping to fell trees and saw logs for the project. A neighbor was surprised to see Victor working alongside others as one of the guys, but it was just what Victor loved about being in camp.

When their own cottage was built, Victor didn't skimp on building materials. He ordered the latest cutting-edge, top-of-the-line

The Weaver cottage at Camp Hebron was a treasured place of retreat and family gatherings. Author's photo.

siding. This new product included insulation in combination with wood. "Use the best" was his byword. Sixty years later, that siding is still holding its own on the Weaver cabin. Victor and son, Dale, took this approach in many things they did. They believed buying quality merchandise was best in the long run. Dale installed a top-of-the-line dishwasher in their new Leola home. It was still running fine when they sold the property years later.

Victor's passion for Camp Hebron went beyond a place of personal retreat. He joined the camp association, served on committees, and financially supported its ministry to children from Mennonite congregations in New York City. These children benefited from the beautiful, peaceful setting and new experiences of this Christian camp atmosphere. One city camper was favorably impressed with the camp except for the pesky gnat flies that were part of the scene. He expressed his feelings thus: "Lord, I like the food and the people here, but these bugs gotta go!" Rural and urban campers alike could agree![11]

Camp Hebron was a place of retreat and relaxation for the Weavers, but they were also involved in camp life and willing to serve when needed. During William Weaver's tenure as Camp Hebron's director, he got to know Victor and Edith very well. He knew he could ask them for help occasionally when additional volunteers were needed. On a particular weekend event, the camp was completely full. William needed additional help to serve the Sunday noon meal.

The Weavers had invited Edith's sister, Irene, and husband Ivan Martin along to the cabin that weekend so William's request had implications for them as well. After hearing of William's need, all four readily agreed to help out.

Younger Mennonite professionals, doctors, lawyers, and corporate business people from the Franconia area, were among the weekend guests. Many knew of these successful, wealthy, Lancaster County business owners of Weaver's Poultry and Martin's Limestone but only by name. As the two couples assisted the serving staff serving, someone recognized their servers. Word began to spread from table to table. People were amazed at what they saw in the service of these unassuming volunteers. William said, "It was very wonderful to see the reactions of the diners when they realized they were being served by those they perceived as part of a 'higher echelon.'" William concluded it was the best example of "servant leadership" for this group to see. It went beyond anything that might have been planned. When their daughter, Janet, heard this story recently, she said it sounded like a typical happening for them.[12]

THE WEAVER COMPANY PICNIC

Melvin Wert's father, Paul, worked for many years at Weaver. The early employee family picnics were held on the company plant grounds. Later picnics were at the Weaver pavilion in the New Holland Park.

At an early picnic at the Weaver plant, young third grader, Melvin, had just won a contest and was running excitedly across the plant courtyard to tell his parents. Suddenly a large cement birdbath loomed directly in front of him. His attempt at hurdling it failed. There was a resounding crash that sent the basin flying as he tumbled to the ground in pain, and the fear "he might have cost his dad his job." Almost immediately he was surrounded by a "soft, gentle caring voice," and inquiries about injury. Mel was amazed to realize that it was the president of the company, Victor himself, there to care for him and allay his fears about his father's job. He was also assured the broken birdbath was of little consequence.

Later, as a teenager working at Weaver, Mel got to know the whole family and experienced the climate of their home as "cheerful and a soft-spoken manner maintained by Edith and daughter Janet." After he washed the Weavers' car at the plant, he always had a generous tip handed to him by "a smiling Edith." Mel and Dale Weaver's friendship deepened during the years they served together on the youth fellowship committee at the New Holland Mennonite Church.[13]

THE DaLa COMPANY

In the late sixties, Victor had an idea that would save the company money. Weaver leased some of its plant and office equipment, such as ice machines and office calculators, from a company at considerable expense. Victor decided to set up his own company and lease equipment to Weaver providing the same service directly. With Dale Weaver and Larry Newswanger, they formed the DaLa Leasing Company.

A Blue Ball National Bank loan provided most of the funding, but Victor and Dale invited a group of friends and associates to invest smaller amounts of money in the company. They wanted to help others gain some experience learning about business and investing. The company was soon paying dividends, and the stock was increasing in value.

DaLa's success gained others' attention. By 1986, the Blue Ball bank considered forming its own leasing company. Other banks were also getting into the leasing business. Whether or not this growing interest could be attributed to Victor's initiative, it was another example of his entrepreneurial skill at work.

Dale Weaver, a Blue Ball board member, suggested that the bank purchase the DaLa Company. The Susquehanna Bank countered Blue Ball bank's offer by fifty percent. Before the transaction could be finalized, there were even higher bids and expressions of interest from banks beyond Lancaster County. When Larry Newswanger suggested that perhaps they see how much higher the price might go, Dale believed the sale price was fair and that they "shouldn't be greedy." The deal with Susquehanna for DaLa became final on September 30, 1986.[14]

CHAPTER 5

The Puerto Rico Connection

HELP WANTED

Following World War II, many Puerto Ricans came to the States out of economic necessity due to the island's high unemployment rate. Many came as contract workers to Lancaster County's tomato farms. US citizenship made their travel to the mainland convenient. Farmers were increasing their tomato acreage to supply the Campbell Soup Company's demand, and consequently had a local worker short-

Fully loaded with three-quarter bushel baskets, a truck is off to the cannery in this 1942 photo from Joseph and Bertha Bucher's Lime Rock farm. The Buchers used an early tomato harvester designed for them by Ben High, but in the 1950s many neighboring farmers hired Puerto Rican laborers who lived in remodeled farm sheds for the harvest season. Used by permission.

age at harvest time. Although Campbell's need was a good problem to have, farmers had to find a solution to the labor shortage. The Puerto Rican influx of the 1950s helped to fill the gap.

As his operation grew, Victor Weaver found Amish and Old Order Mennonite communities to be a good source of labor. Although these groups had an excellent work ethic, they took off from work in large numbers for social occasions such as weddings and funerals. Due to this phenomenon, at certain times of the year, it became difficult for Weaver to maintain full-time production.[1]

Hispanic workers became the stabilizing element of Weaver's workforce. Weaver became the first major employer in Lancaster County to hire Hispanics as full-time workers. Ross Esbenshade was the connecting link to this new source of labor. He and Victor were friends. They were in the same Sunday School class. Ross suggested to Victor that he consider hiring Puerto Ricans who found their seasonal employment in the tomato harvest unsatisfactory. Permanent jobs led to growth of the local Hispanic community. Victor drew criticism from some in the community for hiring Puerto Ricans. They believed he was taking advantage of these new arrivals as cheap labor for his business, but he showed a great deal of interest in them beyond just processing his chickens.

In the years of harvesting tomatoes, temporary housing was often substandard. Some lived in places such as a damp, tobacco strip-

Rohrer farm, about 1955. These seasonal tomato workers were hosted on the farm of Clarence and Alverta Rohrer, 2508 Creek Hill Road, Lancaster, PA. The living quarters for these men were in the tobacco shed, and here they pose by two of their beds. Used by permission.

ping room. A few were fortunate enough to occupy rooms in the owner's farmhouse. Housing was also an issue in the early years of full-time employment at Weaver. The need was so great that some lived temporarily in renovated Weaver chicken houses. Like language barriers, this situation needed improvement.[2]

A JOB AND A CHURCH

With full-time employment at Weaver, a growing Hispanic population took on more permanence in New Holland. A Spanish-language Sunday School class and preaching service at New Holland Mennonite Church was the beginning of the first Hispanic Mennonite Church of the Lancaster Mennonite Conference. The growing fellowship rented a basement room in Kauffman's Hardware Store on Main Street. The historic remains of the town's early primitive jail could still be seen in the basement next to the room used for church.

These steps lead to the basement of Kauffman's Hardware Store on Main Street in New Holland where the Spanish Mennonite Church began. Photo by author.

William Lauver, who served the Spanish Mennonite community as pastor, believed Victor treated his workers fairly. He recognized the difficulties of hiring Latinos and keeping a business running
smoothly. Language obstacles and cultural issues such as punctuality,
or just showing up daily for work were some of the issues. William
felt that Victor wanted to give people a chance to earn a living and be
successful here in the states.[3]

In 1955, Lauver preached his first Spanish sermon there. His
Spanish-speaking ability was an asset to the work of the church and
to Victor Weaver. Victor called him at times to help translate with
language difficulties they were unable to resolve at the plant.

Behind the scenes, others were asking William for a different
kind of help. Local Anglo-Mennonite women considering marriage
to Hispanics had an important question in that era for him: What
does the Bible teach about marrying someone of another race? As
he counseled these women or a couple ask-
ing for help, his reply was that he "couldn't
find any biblical prohibition" against such
a union, but he went on to address the cultural realities. He tried to help the woman
understand the traditional male role of leadership in the Latino family and the social
difficulties they and their children would
encounter in a society not yet open to such
arrangements. As he reflected later on these
marriages, he believed that most succeeded,
but even the best marriages had to struggle
with the cultural and social realities.[4]

From its beginning, Victor supported
the Spanish Mennonite Church. He invested a significant amount of time and money
on the project. In 1975, when the New Holland Mennonite Church moved to its new

*William Lauver served the
Spanish Mennonite congre-
gation during its early years
in New Holland. He spoke
Spanish very well. Victor
sometimes relied on him to
help untangle language difficulties at the plant.* Courtesy
of Lester Blank.

building on the western edge of town, the Hispanic congregation purchased the old, downtown building. Victor served on the Renovation Committee for eighteen months assisting in planning needed renovations in heating, electric and plumbing. He was also instrumental in raising and contributing to the $50,000 needed for the project.[5]

Weaver also supported this growing congregation by hiring church leaders and pastors. Although not originally licensed or ordained, George Gonzales also assisted with Spanish sermons and was heavily involved in the work. He worked for 30 years at Weaver as a knife sharpener in the cut-up department. Sharp knives were in constant demand for workers. They didn't have time to sharpen knives as they worked butchering chickens on the moving disassembly line. George, and others like him, kept their steels busy providing the necessary sharp knives. But as his hands were busy, George kept his ears open. He listened and observed the workplace atmosphere. He challenged racial discrimination directly or addressed it to those above him. He had a close relationship with Victor and could go directly to the top if such concerns weren't addressed.

George could also call Victor regarding islanders' plans for coming to the mainland. By the time they arrived, provision for their employment at Weaver was already in the works. Weaver found it beneficial to the company and to growing local Hispanic Mennonite congregations to hire other pastors at Weaver for similar roles.[6]

Victor Weaver took a personal interest in his workers. Walking through the plant, he stopped to chat with Latino and other workers. He modeled the need to nurture a positive relationship with this new labor force. With his leadership, Ben Burkholder, John Kennel, Melvin Mitchell, Luke Bomberger and others embodied this top-down approach. They recognized that people new to this culture and language needed help to become effective workers and members of the community. What was good for their workers, was good for Weaver. This enlightened approach took form in specific policies.

A NEW LANGUAGE AND CULTURE

Workers of different cultural backgrounds cautiously explored their differences. Some Amish parents feared close association with Puerto Rican workers and didn't permit young people to work at Weaver. As Amish workers moved beyond their reservations, some parents invited these newcomers to share meals in their homes.

Ramona Rivera Santiago remembers a young Amish girl's courage to voice a common stereotype. She asked, "Is it true that all Puerto Ricans carry knives?" Her fears were not allayed by Ramona's mischievous reply, "Yeah, you should see the one in my purse!" But Hispanics had their own impressions as well. Observing the close association of Latino workers and local Mennonite churches, the rumor spread that one had to become a Mennonite if you wanted a job at Victor Weaver's! Although this wasn't true, it was a reasonable assumption. Many Hispanics were becoming part of the Mennonite community in New Holland.[7]

Tina Hess Glanzer with a Puerto Rican family who lived on their property and became family friends. Courtesy of Tina Hess Glanzer.

Tina Hess Glanzer remembers a Puerto Rican family, the Valentins, who lived on their small farm. On the outskirts of New Holland, the farm owned by John H. Hess Sr. and his wife, Elsie, was close to Victor Weaver's plant. The family lived in a Quonset hut on the Hess property, and soon the families became friends.

A Halloween incident one night illustrated how much the Valentins had to learn of mainland culture. John decided to have a bit of fun scaring the family in a Halloween costume. Unfamiliar with this event, the Valentins feared the perceived apparition was a ghost from the dead. Chagrined, John found it a teachable moment for both families.

When John and Elsie sold their farm to New Holland Machine Company, Hess bought a home in a wooded area just outside New Holland for rental to the Valentin family. When people expressed fear their chickens might not be safe with such neighbors, John bought another place for the family in town, and the Hess family moved to the house in the woods. The two families continued their friendship and visited each other in their homes. As a child, Tina fondly remembers a meal of *Arroz con Pollo* at the Valentin home, and she still enjoys the dish and memories today.

Boyd Wert worked in a supervisory role with Hispanics and took a keen interest in them. His commitment to learn Spanish illustrated his deep desire to relate to these workers. His son, Nelson, remembers the Wert family and others being invited to a Hispanic family's home for a pig roast.[8]

Although there were some grumblings about the number of Latinos in the community, and the company heard some of these complaints, such feelings didn't spill over into overt acts of opposition. The New Holland community pool was one place these increasingly negative feelings came into focus. A few residents voiced their distress to pool management with this solution: Could the park simply deny admission to these people? But they were reminded by park officials that these were American citizens, and the request was untenable. The pool would remain open to all.[9]

John H. Hess Sr. with two Hispanic friends. Courtesy of Tina Hess Glanzer.

Francisco Delgado Jr. arrived on the mainland from Puerto Rico in 1955. After he graduated from high school, he couldn't find much job potential in Puerto Rico. In 1953, two of his older brothers had already come to the States. He followed them to New Holland and Victor Weaver's plant. He and others lived in a "small house" on the property for six months at no cost. Francisco isn't sure, but the house he lived in may have been one of the converted chicken houses briefly in use. After that, he rented a room in town until he married. Francisco's parents and sisters never moved to the United States.

For the young Francisco, New Holland was a welcoming town. He enjoyed hanging out with friends on weekend evenings without incident. He said, "People were nice here. There was no trouble." Coming to the States had been a good decision. When he first arrived, he was surprised by the straight roads and ease of travel. In Puerto Rico, the roads were bad. On many winding roads, one had to stop and blow the horn to be sure no truck was coming around the bend, before moving ahead.

Francisco soon had a job at Weaver. Before machines were used, everything was done by hand and took longer. He remembers working until 9 or 10 o'clock some evenings. Francisco learned some English in Puerto Rico but it didn't sound like what was spoken here in the States. He didn't attend any of the language classes offered at Weaver. He learned English on the job and acknowledged that some of the Spanish words he heard used here had quite different meanings in Puerto Rico. Francisco's work experience was similar to others— some remained at Weaver all their working lives—while others like Francisco, who worked at Weaver for 8 years, moved on to other jobs and worked as a mechanic for many years.

Francisco first met Arlene Good at a New Holland softball league game. Arlene's brother played for the New Holland team and Francisco was part of the Weaver team. They dated and married when Arlene was 19. Apparently Arlene's sisters were impressed with Francisco—four of them also married Puerto Rican men!

Arlene Good Delgado began working at Weaver in 1966 when she was 17 years old. She didn't follow her husband's lead to other jobs. She stayed at Weaver for 50 years, working in many departments during that time. She agreed there was a spirit of family at Weaver. Like Victor, other people were very friendly. People in management like Ben Burkholder, John Kennel and John Weaver didn't let their higher positions keep them from relating to workers.

Francisco remembers Victor inviting Latinos to his home on several occasions for coffee and cookies. He said, "Victor talked about church and the Bible." Francisco soon became involved with the Spanish Mennonite Church beginning in New Holland. Others went to the Catholic church in town.

Francisco and Arlene have lived in a development near New Holland for 40 years. Their life together is a good example of how the Puerto Rico connection brought many here who settled in and became part of their local communities.[10]

Prior to working at Weaver, tomato farmers and their workers' language difficulties could lead to serious misunderstandings. One farmer almost lost his whole workforce over the inability to communicate about a simple request. The workers wanted to buy lard they used in cooking, but the farmer couldn't understand what the men were trying to tell him. The workers' frustration became so great that they were tempted to pack up and leave. In these situations,

Francisco Delgado Jr. and his wife, Arlene Good Delgado, met at a league softball game in New Holland. Courtesy of Francisco and Arlene Delgado.

only Spanish-speaking church leaders were able to help.

Victor recognized the problems of language differences. He asked T. K. Hershey to step into this gap. Hershey's long-term ministry to Hispanics uniquely qualified him to bridge the cultural-language divide. In addition to his ministry, Hershey developed a Spanish-language workers' manual useful in times when communication was difficult. Availability of others fluent in both languages also helped resolve work communications. In her office job, Ramona Rivera Santiago's assistance helped smooth the way when understanding wasn't clear.[11]

T. K. Hershey's Spanish Language Manual helped new workers to understand basic information about their work and the Weaver organization. Courtesy of New Holland Area Historical Society.

Language misunderstandings could create serious problems in labor relationships. In the Personnel Department, John Kennel hired a recently returned missionary to help address language challenges. Relying on his Spanish learned in Central America, the former missionary made a public address announcement in Spanish. As workers listened, many of them were ready to walk out of the plant in protest. Although not understood at the time, the Spanish spoken in Central America included words with very different meanings compared to their usage in Puerto Rico, and what the returned missionary was saying was very offensive. After management understood the perceived insult, John Kennel quickly defused the situation. A prompt apology and explanation reassured workers of the intended message.[12]

In addition to development of the Spanish job manual, Weaver sponsored English classes and printed some articles of its monthly employee magazine, *Poultry Lines,* in Spanish. This company newsletter included jobs available and work promotions. These were concrete illustrations of Weaver's intention to treat all employees with respect, regardless of racial or cultural backgrounds. As the company grew, more formalized programs continued to address language needs.

In 1982, Weaver offered a refresher course in English called "Practical English and the Command of Words." Training and Development Manager, Harold Stauffer, was pleased with the response to the course. Most of the students were salaried and clerical workers.

A year later, the company offered a more comprehensive language class. While most participants were Latinos, others also benefited. The Industrial English course aimed to assist workers experiencing culture shock in a new country and language barriers making work more difficult. Exploring American customs and history helped students gain more understanding of American culture.

Employees involved in all aspects of poultry processing at Weaver were also part of the class. The class was relevant to many job situations workers might encounter, as well as aspects of job safety. In-house instructor, Hernando Aviles, helped Latino students feel more comfortable with their learning task. Personnel manager, Larry Brown, the first African American hired in the Human Resource Department, emphasized improving English skills as essential to better

The English taught in this class was job related. The goal was to help Hispanic employees increase their speaking and writing abilities. Courtesy of New Holland Area Historical Society.

job performance and opportunities for advancement. Its program was likely the first of its kind offered by any industry in Lancaster County.[13]

When Larry Brown graduated from Goshen College with a major in Spanish, he hoped to teach, but life experiences took him in an entirely different direction. In 1976, the Weaver company was looking for a bilingual, Spanish-speaking person. After his interview, Larry took the job despite a pay cut. He headed for what his puzzled city friends in Cleveland, Ohio, called "that chicken place." In Lancaster County, he found a different, more rural culture to figure out and join. That might have helped him become more sympathetic to Hispanic employees' culture shock when they arrived in New Holland. In addition to speaking the language, Victor emphasized the importance of relating to the Spanish culture with respect, honesty and professionalism.

Brown understood the machismo aspect of Hispanic culture as

Larry Brown was the first African-American hired in the Human Resource Department. Courtesy of Larry Brown.

he dealt with employee altercations. With no need for a translator, he communicated freely with those involved in a respectful manner to preserve their dignity, but he also helped them acknowledge violation of company policy and the need to resolve the situation.

The importance of family was a deeply-rooted trait of Puerto Rican culture. If a family member had an emergency such as illness, a worker might stay home for days without informing supervisors of their situation, or simply take off to be with sick family members back in Puerto Rico. In an industry with a perishable product, such absenteeism made it difficult for the poultry operation to run effectively. The labor of Puerto Ricans and others of color, helped Weaver resolve its labor force needs, but it was not without continued effort to acclimate newcomers into the system to keep turning out the product.[14]

A VISIT FROM THE ARMSTRONG CORPORATION

In the 1970s, Weaver's Human Resource Department had two bilingual employees. Although modest by today's standards, it was progressive for that time as illustrated by a visit from Armstrong Corporation's human resources staff. Armstrong, a Fortune 500 company located in Lancaster, visited Weaver to learn about a problem that they couldn't solve: How did Weaver attract and keep people of color in its workforce? After some time in conversation, a Weaver executive asked the Armstrong staff the defining question: "How many bilingual people do you have in personnel?" With none in their department, it soon became evident where Armstrong could begin to address the problem.

Allon H. Lefever's personal motto of treating every person with dignity echoed Victor Weaver's own beliefs he shared with others in management positions. Weaver's programs were a concrete way of regarding people with dignity and respect for their unique heritage. The visit gave Armstrong a practical example to follow.[15]

CHAPTER 6

The Era of Prepared Foods, 1970-1980s

SUCCESS OF THE CHICKEN ROLL AND A CHANGE OF COURSE

As Executive Vice President, Dale M. Weaver gave leadership to the team's development of new Weaver products. The continued success of their Weaver Chicken Roll became the catalyst for change. Victor and his team saw prepared foods as the wave of the future. The company prepared for a change of direction.

As an entrepreneur who often saw the future a step or two ahead of others, sometimes Victor had to wait for the public to catch up with his vision and for changes in technology. In 1946 Victor offered breaded, fried chicken as a prepared food but the public wasn't buying it. However, consumer behaviors were changing.

Changes in technology were opening the door of acceptance to frozen, prepared foods. Melvin Mitchell noted that before the 1960s, most people didn't have refrigerators with adequate freezers to store frozen foods. In those days, many people rented space in a local frozen food locker several miles from home. They left the bulk of their frozen foods in these walk-in lockers and took small amounts home to use. Now, newer refrigerators offered larger, better freezers for home use, ending this inconvenience, and making prepared foods more attractive.

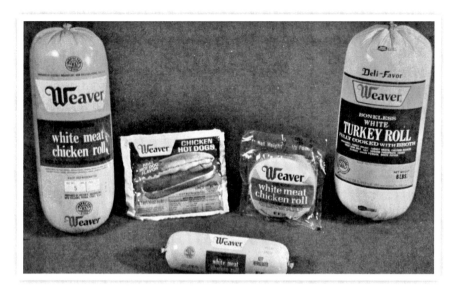

Popularity of the Weaver Chicken Roll convinced Victor the public was now ready for prepared frozen foods and deli items. Courtesy of New Holland Area Historical Society.

BETTER BATTER FROZEN FRIED CHICKEN

Despite better home freezers, companies were having little success selling their frozen fried chicken to American consumers. Weaver's Product Development department, led by Dale Weaver, decided to take on the challenge. His eventual success didn't come easily. Work to accomplish this goal would take most of the decade to perfect the product and to sell the public on the idea.

Dale began the research to develop a superior frozen fried chicken product with appeal to northern tastes. The first major hurdle was work perfecting the batter. Early attempts were unsatisfactory. The batter had to provide a consistent, complete coating. In addition to the quality of coverage, a tasty product was crucial. Eventually, they consulted the Golden Dipped Company. Its tempura batter was being used on seafood and it had several desirable qualities. In addition to its adhesive quality, the tempura batter gave it a special, crispy bite, and it was easy to flavor. There were important details to be refined for the production line, but they were resolved.

The product was ready, but was the public? Weaver emphasized the *precooked* aspect of their chicken to separate it from raw, frozen chicken parts that had been around for a long time but never caught on. Chicken drive-ins were making fried chicken more acceptable to the northern palate accustomed to roasted chicken. Precooked chicken suggested convenient preparation at home, and television commercials also stressed the convenience of preparation. More appealing packaging gained attention. By the late sixties, major companies like Banquet, Swanson and Morton were convinced Weaver had accomplished a real breakthrough in prepared frozen foods. They soon jumped on the bandwagon.[2]

New products continued to roll off the Weaver line in the seventies. Dutch Frye chicken provided a different taste with more crispy batter and spice. Chicken croquettes, pies, turnovers and chicken au gratin followed.

In 1974, Weaver "reinvented" the hot dog using chicken instead of beef. Weaver's chicken hot dogs won top honors with a nutritional plus of 20% fewer calories per ounce and 22% less fat than traditional hot dogs. Kunzler and Company, Inc., a local meat processing company in Lancaster, Pennsylvania, assisted Weaver in production of the new hot dog.

Melvin Mitchell described the inception of the chicken hot dog as a "tough sell" for traditionally-minded consumers. As people

A Weaver breakthrough with its prepared frozen fried chicken soon had major competitors scrambling to catch up. Advertising on the television show, "Let's Make a Deal," and others, helped to attract consumers.
Courtesy of New Holland Area Historical Society.

became more conscious of a healthy diet, the product gained more of a following. Bill Pellman worked hard in sales to get the product moving.

Weaver plant expansion reflected a growing demand for a variety of products. A new 85,000-square foot building was nearly finished. It would complete what Edith Weaver had suggested years before with her question "Why not put the whole area of operations under one roof?" That would soon be a reality. Now 100,000 chickens could be processed daily by over 1,500 employees. Weaver's modest beginning was difficult to imagine; now it was one of the largest employers in Lancaster County.[3]

Michael Good began employment at Weaver in the early seventies and worked his way up to line supervisor. He described Weaver as a well-run family business with an established New England market niche and other East Coast area markets. He remained with the company through its transition of succeeding ownerships. He became plant manager under Holly Farms, and Tyson's complex manager.[4]

ADVERTISING TO INFLUENCE CONSUMER TASTES

With Weaver products successfully launched, advertising was the next step of marketing strategy. In 1971, the company started regional advertising with ads on television, in newspapers and magazines. The Weaver brand became known and established in the eastern United States. Exports and food service markets became additional outlets for Weaver products in places as distant as Europe and Japan.

Melvin Mitchell concentrated on television commercials and other ads to educate the public. The company turned to top advertising agencies in New York and Los Angeles to craft quality ads. Mel made many trips to Los Angeles to ensure commercials were "proper and honest." With its ad—"Come On Up To Northern Fried Chicken"—Weaver hoped to attract notice and increase sales.[5]

GROWING PAINS

In September 1979, an article called "Growing Pains" in the in-house employees' magazine, *Weaver Poultry Lines*, addressed some of the ways the company had changed in the past decade. There were some pains of inconvenience including employees' long walk from the parking lot, and the need to show their Weaver identity badges to the newly hired security service. Those working late into the evening or arriving at the plant on weekends felt their long-standing belonging at Weaver being challenged by security inquiries. Crowded locker and lunchroom facilities added to frustrations.

But employees were also experiencing issues more significant than inconvenience. Some feared getting lost in the "bigness" of the company. With sales volume now three times greater and production departments expanded, new facilities and equipment brought changes in work schedules and communication.

In the past, line supervisors knew their superiors on a first-name basis. Now there were more layers of management. Personnel manager, Jim Roth, observed that the specialization in areas of data processing and commodities analysis made one-on-one communications difficult.

For a business to function well as it grows, at some point there must be a transition from the simpler "entrepreneurial stage," to a more sophisticated "professional management" approach. In the entrepreneurial stage at Weaver, employees' work roles were less complicated and relationships more direct. In many ways, professionalization put more distance between the founder and his workers, but Victor's continued relationship with employees helped counterbalance the dynamic of change.[6]

In the *Weaver Poultry Lines*, Allon Lefever, Vice President of Corporate Planning and Economic Research, wrote that Weaver's growth intensified the dynamics of their operation. Changes in the marketplace had a more rapid, direct impact. Problems affected more people, money and sales, with greater risk to profit and loss. Adjust-

Later, Weaver's Rondelet Chicken Pattie became another popular prepared food. Its "down-home flavor" was designed to compete with the taste of fast-food chicken. Courtesy of New Holland Area Historical Society.

ments to meet these challenges would take more time than in the past. Growing pains such as these, Lefever said, ". . . make production and marketing infinitely more complex."

Prompt product distribution service, a Weaver hallmark, was another part of this complexity. Customers computerized their inventories to reduce the amount of money tied up in warehouse stock, but when they needed products, they expected a quick response. With Weaver's market area stretching west as far as St. Louis, Missouri, and south to Florida, new patterns of distribution and the costs of transportation were additional challenges.[7]

Employees were reminded that growth is necessary or a business will decline; Weaver was no longer the small, intimate company it once was. It was growing out of the little league, not quite in the big leagues yet, but it would soon consider actions to become a national player.

Growing pains weren't only the concern of employees; Victor became aware of his own growing prominence and feelings of personal vulnerability. Fearing robbery, he started carrying $300 in a special wallet he was prepared to surrender quickly with the hope an assailant would take the money and run. He also kept this cash on hand at home when answering the front door. An intercom system installed at the door was another precaution for meeting whomever was on the other side.[8]

Victor was most comfortable being anonymous. When dining out with a local businessman friend, he was startled when the friend drew an acquaintance passing their table into their conversation and introduced Victor as "the Victor Weaver." When they were alone again, Victor voiced his discomfort saying, "Don't ever do that again!" To the friend, "he seemed almost paranoid."[9]

But there were times when Victor seemed to relax and enjoy spending money in a public setting for a good cause. He was comfortable among friends at benefit auctions for church schools, camps and other such organizations he supported. After purchasing a quilt at a school auction, he said, "Sell it again," and enjoyed the excitement this created. It was a way of giving back to community causes he believed in.

LEADERSHIP FOR THE NEXT GENERATION

As Victor grew older and experienced some concerns about his health, he looked to the future and who would give leadership to his company. When Victor considered choosing his son Dale, who grew up in the family business to succeed him, he also consulted other family members about their interest in joining the leadership team. Son-in-law, Larry Newswanger, and Victor had several conversations about Larry's future plans after graduation from college. Larry was a junior at Birmingham Southern College when Victor, now in his sixties, invited him to become part of the transition team with Dale's leadership. There was no pressure, and Victor simply shared his desire to keep ownership within the family. During Larry's senior year in

1967, Victor and Edith visited again. Now more pressing than future leadership, the company needed additional operating capital to grow, but didn't want financial needs to compromise the values of their family-owned business or its leadership.

Although Larry and Janet declined the offer to become part of Weaver, they were grateful for the consideration given to them. After graduation, Larry wanted to use his skills in church-related work. His decision to accept the position as Secretary of Personnel/Office manager of Eastern Mennonite Board of Missions and Charities in 1967 still benefitted Victor. It had become the practice for Victor and other Lancaster area businesspeople to balance Eastern Board's budget at the end of a fiscal year. They contributed substantial funds to that effect. Now Larry provided access to monthly financial statements giving Victor an on-going understanding related to these end-of-year requests.

Grandson Greg Newswanger was also consulted. He recalls a brief conversation at a Sunday family gathering. Sometime before the sale of the company to Holly Farms, Dale and Victor wondered aloud whether they should "save the company for him." Still in college and lacking a clear career direction, he was reluctant to make such a significant commitment.[10]

Delbert Seitz believed that as Victor approached retirement years, he wanted to help Dale build a younger, professionally trained management team for the future. When Victor began his business with an eighth-grade education, he hired Ben Burkholder, Melvin Mitchell and others with similar backgrounds. They grew with the company to become part of his inner management circle. Surrounded by this core of good people with their inherent abilities and Victor's entrepreneurial vision, the company prospered during its first 40 years. But the time was coming to pass that mantle to a younger generation.

Allon Lefever graduated from The Pennsylvania State University with a master's degree in Economics. His special interest was money and banking, but he decided to join the Weaver management team in 1974 and left the banking option for later. He was the first of the

Allon Lefever's star rose rapidly at Weaver. He became Vice President of Operations when Ben Burkholder retired. Courtesy of Allon H. Lefever.

"young kids" to join Dale Weaver's team as Director of Corporate Planning and Forecasting. His talents were soon put to use.

In the early seventies, the shortfall of grain production in the Soviet Union led to huge grain purchases and global prices soared. When the price of corn doubled, Weaver became concerned. Grain prices were important to Weaver's cost of feeding their broiler flocks. The company needed a hedging plan to insure predictable future costs for corn and soybeans. Allon got the task and a promotion to Commodity Analyst. This position put Allon in close contact with Victor and Dale. Victor checked commodity prices daily and as part of his job, Allon reported to Dale. When Ben Burkholder was nearing retirement, Dale promoted 33-year-old Allon as the next Vice President of Operations. Other duties such as purchasing were added to Allon's responsibilities.

Allon was impressed with Victor's management team and their sophisticated planning. As operations chief, Allon was in charge of product production; Vice President of Sales, Mel Mitchell, worked closely with Lefever. Weaver employed talented people and and made significant investments in research, development, automation, and equipment to create a more advanced organization ahead of many others.[11]

HEALTH

Victor's responsibility to keep a growing business on track in a competitive economy had its stressful times. When he felt the anxiety of work-related issues, he looked to others for help. When Victor consulted Bishop J. Paul Graybill for his counsel, he found it difficult for the churchman to appreciate the context of business issues. Victor found more encouragement relating to other business people on the Philhaven board. His empathy for people in business sometimes motivated him to share from his own experiences with others. One such opportunity happened just outside his office door when Victor shared his concern regarding the importance of good business organization and its effect on personal health.

Calvin High and his father Sanford of High Welding Company, were setting up their 40-ton crane in preparation to work on a Weaver building project. Victor was troubled by what he observed. As the Highs worked, Victor approached Calvin and said, "I want to see you in my office." When Calvin arrived, Victor closed the door and got directly to the point. "Do you and your father own this firm?" After High's affirmative reply, Victor wondered why Calvin was working at the job site. Victor said, "I used to think I could do everything, too; you must learn to delegate responsibilities or you will end up on the floor just as I did!" He urged Calvin to manage the bigger picture of their company from his office and to delegate responsibilities to others.

Calvin was impressed by this gesture of concern. "He talked to me in private; it meant a lot to me as a young person in those early days of our business." Such assertiveness, not Victor's usual style, indicated the depth of his concern and moved him beyond his usual reserve to share a word of counsel. Although it isn't clear what medical incident in Victor's past he was referring to, he did have a history of heart-related issues.[12]

GOING PUBLIC

Delbert Seitz joined Weaver management at a critical time. He learned from Dale Weaver that Luke Bomberger was leaving his position as company controller. The two met at an Eastern Mennonite College alumni function. Dale encouraged Delbert to apply for the job, and Seitz's interest grew with the news that Weaver was preparing to "go public"—selling stock to the public for operating capital. Seitz, trained in all aspects of accounting and finance, wanted to be part of the action in such a business situation. He hoped to build ownership in a public business by purchasing stock and acquiring shares as part of his compensation.

This initial public offering, or IPO, can raise operating capital for a company's growth. But such an endeavor isn't simple. The commodities' market volatility, an important factor when assessing a poultry company's worth, makes assessment difficult. Competition and market penetration are also critical aspects.

In 1971, Weaver's significant negative balance of operating capital reinforced this financial need. The following year the company offered a prospectus in preparation of an IPO known as a "red herring." The front page of such a document states in bold red print that the information given is preliminary and will be updated on the offering date. This trial balloon tests investors' interest and is useful in application to the Securities and Exchange Commission. However, at the last minute, Victor squelched the undertaking. He believed the company was being undervalued and would not have the desired appeal needed for an IPO.

Victor's decision not to go through with this effort may have been due to financial information gathered within the company while preparing the prospectus. Public companies with consistent value and predictable profits are most attractive. A five-year financial projection of profits ending in 1970 revealed Weaver anticipated more robust profits than actual sales and cost structure supported for those years. Although the returns during those years were adequate, they were not at the level anticipated.

Seitz stated that from his experience working for two poultry companies, there is difficulty in making a consistent profit in this business. Major companies' size and diversification can make them less susceptible to the fluctuations of commodities and other market factors, but they also experience these problems.

PRELIMINARY PROSPECTUS DATED NOVEMBER 3, 1972

PROSPECTUS

250,000 Shares

Weaver.

Victor F. Weaver, Inc.

Common Stock

Of these shares, 230,762 are being sold by the Company and 19,238 by certain share-holders named under "Selling Shareholders". Prior to this offering, there has been no public market for the Common Stock. The initial public offering price has been determined by agreement among the Company, the Selling Shareholders and the Underwriters.

THESE SECURITIES HAVE NOT BEEN APPROVED OR DISAPPROVED BY THE SECURITIES AND EXCHANGE COMMISSION NOR HAS THE COMMISSION PASSED UPON THE ACCURACY OR ADEQUACY OF THIS PROSPECTUS. ANY REPRESENTATION TO THE CONTRARY IS A CRIMINAL OFFENSE.

	Price to Public	Underwriting Discount(1)	Proceeds to Company(2)	Proceeds to Selling Shareholders(2)
Per Share	$	$	$	$
Total (3)	$	$	$	$

(1) See "Underwriting" for information concerning indemnification of the Underwriters.

(2) Before deducting expenses estimated at $129,225 payable by the Company and $10,775 payable by the Selling Shareholders.

(3) The Company has granted the Underwriters an option, exercisable for 30 days after the date of this Prospectus, to purchase at the Price to Public, less the Underwriting Discount, up to 25,000 additional shares solely to cover over-allotments in the sale of the shares offered hereby. If this option is exercised in full, the total Price to Public, Underwriting Discount and Proceeds to Company will be increased to $, $ and $, respectively.

These shares are offered by the several Underwriters, subject to prior sale, when, as and if delivered to and accepted by them, and subject to the approval of certain legal matters and to certain other conditions.

W. E. HUTTON & CO.   JANNEY MONTGOMERY SCOTT INC.

The date of this Prospectus is November   , 1972

The face page of "Red Herring" prospectus November 3, 1972.
Courtesy of the Newswanger family.

Del Seitz anticipated Weaver going public. When that didn't happen, he helped the company secure a line of operating credit. Courtesy of New Holland Area Historical Society.

Shortly after Seitz joined Weaver in the fall of 1972, he helped the company find another solution to its capital needs. He worked to establish sources of credit. "We always had money to operate," he said. Philadelphia attorney John Esty helped Delbert set up a major line of credit with Central Penn Bank of Philadelphia done with financial covenants Weaver could meet. Seitz also encouraged Weaver to include local banks, Blue Ball National Bank, Farmers' National Bank of New Holland, and Fulton National Bank of Lancaster, in its financial dealings. Money to operate had other implications as well. Victor's financial planning included willingly sharing some of his profits with worthy causes.

A VISION BEYOND THE BOTTOM LINE

Near the end of each fiscal year, Seitz met with Dale, Victor and his administrative assistant, Martha Myers, to plan the company's contributions. Philhaven Hospital, Eastern Mennonite Board of Missions and Charities, and New Holland Community Park were some of the constants on the list. Weaver also supported the Welsh Mountain Clinic. In addition to funding the clinic, with Victor's encouragement, Delbert Seitz served on its board for several years before he left the company in 1979.[13]

Eastern Mennonite College became another recipient of Weaver's giving when the EMC administration building was destroyed by fire. Mennonite businesspeople in Lancaster County got a strong appeal for help—the future of EMC and its mission were in jeopardy if the college failed to rebuild. The Weavers pledged $100,000 over five years. They also created scholarship funds at EMC, Goshen College and Elizabethtown College for employees and their children. The Victor F. Weaver Pennsylvania Endowed Scholarship program at EMC began in the 1970s with $25,000 and has grown through investments to more than $100,000. Victor's financial support was gracious even though he felt some members of the institution gave mixed messages to business people.

In his role as an EMC board member, Victor was sensitive to his lack of higher education. Negative messages at the college about business people contributed to his brevity of service on the board. On one occasion he was disturbed by a faculty member's address criticizing the capitalist system, its profit motive, the materialism and greed of people in business. Equally disturbing was a remark that the college was out to "get" Lancaster County's wealthy Mennonite millionaires' [money].

While Victor likely didn't express his discomfort about these anti-business messages, other Harrisonburg business people did speak up. As supporters of the college, they felt such criticisms did little to affirm their identity and work. Although the college had a good accounting department, it would need a strong business department with a Christian business philosophy to keep their support.

When John Eby took on this challenge, he began developing relationships with local business leaders. He invited them to the campus for breakfast seminars and the exchange of ideas. Input from some of these connections was helpful in shaping the college's business philosophy. Professor Eby summarized that philosophy in the September 1985 issue of *The Marketplace*, the Mennonite Economic Development Associates' magazine. In his article, "Entrepreneurship: A Risk, An Honor, A Challenge," Eby clearly addressed the cloud of suspicion many Mennonite businesspeople perceived from others—can a Christian be a business person? It was a question Victor Weaver would address at some point in his life, but long before Eby's address, Victor embodied the values Eby set forth as he built the Weaver company.

Eby acknowledged the risks people take when investing their resources to produce a product for market. If successful, the rewards of profit can pose the danger of becoming greedy, self-centered, and insensitive to the needs of others. On the other hand, successful businesses create jobs; churches and communities benefit in many ways when the bounty of profit is shared and excessive lifestyles are avoided. With such Christ-centered commitment, Eby declared Christian entrepreneurship to be a clearly honorable calling, and their influence can go beyond their own establishments. Christians can promote the high ethical standards they instill in their own companies as examples and a challenge to the whole business community. The high standards of Victor's company were recognized by the poultry industry at the national level.

Eby also spoke about the role of Christians in business at Mennonite Economic Development Association meetings and other such opportunities to present his philosophy. His writing was an eloquent presentation of a positive message about Christians' involvement in business. He summed up the presentation this way:

> *Business entrepreneurship is an expression of the resources that are part of a meaningful life. Christian entrepreneurs show their faith in the economic sector as they live and work there under the lordship of Jesus Christ. They use their energy and creativity, not only to become successful businesspersons, but to incarnate faithful stewardship in relationships and structures of the economic sector.[14]*

TECHNOLOGY AND INVENTION

As Dale Weaver looked to the future, he believed the company should utilize technology to the fullest. He promoted a state-of-the-art computer network at Weaver. This system centralized all company information at New Holland.

Victor also had an inventive mind. He frequently took his ideas and needs to his Engineering Department. Although many were not formally trained as engineers, they had the ability to create the machinery needed on the production lines. Dale believed increased automation was important for the company's future. His desire for robotics sometimes stretched automation to the limits of what was available or possible. Automation for the Cut-up Department's processing line was one example of their creativity being pushed to the limit.

Eugene Martin filled a significant role at this time. Prior to joining Weaver, Martin did his first project for Victor. He designed a machine capable of making wood shavings from green timber. The company believed the moisture in these green wood shavings gave young chicks a better developmental start. Victor asked Eugene to make him such a shavings machine, and Martin delivered a machine that pleased Victor.

The planer he built could reduce a twenty-foot log into the desired shavings in a short time. These shavings carpeted the floors of Weaver's broiler houses, a trend that influenced other growers as well, and led to the formation of the Denver Wood Products company. Victor offered Eugene a job he couldn't refuse—come to New Holland and help build a chicken processing company. Eugene gave birth to many of Victor's mechanical ideas and needs.

Eugene supervised Weaver's Machine Development Department in the seventies. Some mornings when he arrived at work, Victor was already sitting by his door with another idea brewing in his mind. Eugene described his inventive mind as "Mr. Weaver's toy." Victor was like a kid at play with his imagination, and he relied on Eugene to make his visions materialize. Weaver often began by saying, "Could you build . . ." and then described what he envisioned. Eugene and his men would build the machine. Eugene's innate skills were an example of what some have described as "blacksmith engineers." These people, without formal training, have the inventive abilities and skills to succeed through trial and error.

Sometimes Victor came with more than just an idea. On one such occasion, he challenged Eugene to figure out how to make his machines do what Victor demonstrated. He cut up a chicken as Eugene watched and laid out the separate parts. Then he asked Eugene to make a machine to do the same. So this project began for the Cut-up Department.

If a machine was used to cut the leg tendons holding the thigh bone in place, it had to make precise cuts to the tendons. If the thigh bone was cut instead, it left broken, jagged edges making the product unappealing to customers. To avoid this problem, the machine was designed to pull chicken joints apart before cutting the tendons. An

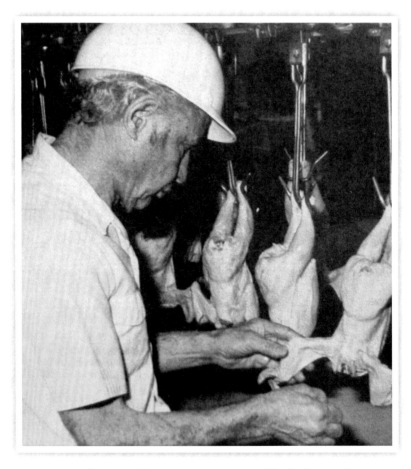

Dave Hess saw many changes in his 20 years of leadership in the Cut-up Department. Courtesy of New Holland Area Historical Society.

United States Patent

Martin et al.

[15] **3,672,000**

[45] **June 27, 1972**

[54] **MACHINE TO DE-BONE CHICKEN THIGHS**

[72] Inventors: **Eugene G. Martin,** Stevens; **Edwin C. Mohler,** Willow Street, both of Pa.

[73] Assignee: **Victor F. Weaver, Inc.,** New Holland, Pa.

[22] Filed: **Aug. 31, 1970**

[21] Appl. No.: **68,260**

[52] U.S. Cl. 17/11, 17/1
[51] Int. Cl. A22c 21/00, A22c 17/04
[58] Field of Search..............................17/1 G, 11, 46

[56] **References Cited**

UNITED STATES PATENTS

3,510,908 5/1970 Segur et al. 17/11
2,893,051 7/1959 Massengill ....17/1 G

Primary Examiner—Lucie H. Laudenslager
Attorney—C. Hercus Just

[57] **ABSTRACT**

A machine for removing the bone from chicken thighs by engaging the ball at one end of the thigh bone and moving stripper members into engagement with the thigh bone immediately below the gripping means, and effecting longitudinal movement between the gripping means and the stripper members until the stripper members move the full length of the bone and engage and move around the ball at the opposite end of the thigh bone, to complete the removal of the meat from said bone.

20 Claims, 17 Drawing Figures

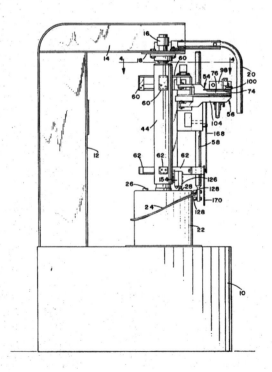

One of Eugene Martin's drawings as part of the patent application process to explain his poultry cut-up machine. Courtesy of Eugene Martin.

additional benefit of this action was saving the "oyster"—pockets of back meat usually left behind by workers manually separating legs from the backbone.

A patent attorney worked closely with the department to advise on patent regulations, areas of possible infringement, and filing patent claims. Victor and Eugene shared some of these patents and proceeds. Eugene felt Victor treated him fairly in this arrangement.

During his work at Weaver, most of Eugene's inventiveness was utilized developing machinery used within the company, but if their cut-up machine was a success, Victor hoped to market it to others. However, the commercial potential wasn't encouraging, and Victor gave up this undertaking. Eugene Martin wanted to continue manufacturing poultry processing equipment. He left Weaver and formed his own FoodCraft company.

Eugene designed several separate machines to perform the operations of their original cut-up machine. In his company work, Eugene gained 28 patents he held alone. His company sold equipment internationally. At home, he said, "Don Tyson and Frank Purdue's companies also became good customers."[15]

Another worker at Weaver, Boyd Wert, built his own gizzard cleaning machine and it was used on the line at Weaver. He decided not to spend the money for a patent and within a few years others designed a similar machine.[16]

Later technology utilizing computers on the production line pushed technology beyond the limits of the Weaver team's inventiveness. A sophisticated machine on line had 18 slots taking in chicken breasts. A computer sorted the slightly different-sized chicken breasts and fed precisely 22 ounces of product into each box at the end of the line. In the past, if a package was an ounce less than the 22 ounces, the company could be in trouble with the government, if the package was overweight by a few ounces, Weaver was losing money.[17]

TROUBLED WATERS

In the 1970s, Weaver faced a difficult dilemma—its daily waste-water was straining the capacity of New Holland borough facilities. Articles in the local press blamed Weaver for environmental dangers to Mill Creek. The creek, described at its best as a "lazy stream" with a low oxygen level, had difficulty sustaining aquatic life. The state fish commission put some trout in Mill Creek to test the water quality—they died within a few minutes!

Weaver believed the solution was a pre-treatment plant to reduce wastewater toxicity before it reached the borough's plant. During construction of this pre-treatment plant, however, a Pennsylvania state court order limited the amount of pre-treated water New Holland was allowed to accept from Weaver. This ruling jeopardized the plant's daily operating capacity and future expansion. Weaver's decided to build a total-water treatment plant. However, when the company looked for other treatment plants to serve as models, they couldn't find any up-to-date system to consult.[18]

The wastewater presented unique challenges. It included a variety of debris requiring special treatment. Feathers, offal, blood, grease, detergent, scraps of cooked and uncooked chicken, caustics, an occasional rubber glove and other surprises might surface.

The plant produced more than a million gallons of wastewater daily. It overwhelmed the borough system in volume and had a toxicity level ten times greater than average household waste. The biochemical oxygen demand, or BOD, a measure of a waste treatment plant's effectiveness breaking down organic material, was alarmingly high. Water entering the treatment plant had an average BOD of 1,000. After treatment, the BOD of 5 was a vast improvement! The water entering Mill Creek was no longer a threat to aquatic life or livestock. Another positive result was that the company discovered a profitable byproduct. The 20,000 pounds of high protein chicken grease extracted weekly from the wastewater could be sold as an ingredient for livestock feed.[19]

Donald Horning, the local Dodge truck and car dealer, was invited to attend the new plant's open house. Plant manager, Leroy Newswanger, proudly conducted tours through this state-of-the-art facility and explained its operation in detail. At the end of the tour, Leroy drew a glass of the processed water and drank it, demonstrating his confidence in what had been accomplished. His longevity didn't appear to suffer; today he is still an energetic senior citizen!

Leroy managed the water treatment plant for over 10 years. Although he didn't have any formal training for the job, he discovered an affinity for its challenges and a "God-given ability" that served him well in this role. When Environmental Protection Association engineers weren't able to help him with problems in the new plant, Leroy devised his own improvements and became articulate in the science of water purification. Leroy even assisted EPA officials in developing regulations for future feather plant operations.

One day when visiting the site, Victor suggested that Leroy display a large fish tank or aquarium using treated water, for visitors to see. Despite all the technical information he gave on tours, Leroy believed the fish tank was his best demonstration of the water's purity. Although he didn't have frequent communication with Victor, he perceived him as a "gentleman highly respected" within his company because of the way he related to his workers.[20]

Leroy Newswanger, a self-taught hydrologist, at work in his lab testing the water quality. Courtesy of New Holland Area Historical Society.

Building the water treatment plant illustrates Victor's community-minded spirit, and his desire to be a good neighbor. He was pleased with the results of this more than a million dollar investment.

The New Holland Clarion warned that expanding the town's treatment system would be costly for its "already tax-burdened citizens." But *The Clarion*'s front-page article also carried good news about Weaver. It was taking action to build a treatment plant to resolve the dilemma and spare the borough residents' more taxes. In the end, what was good for Weaver was also good for his neighbors. The company's operation and future planning were no longer in jeopardy.[21]

PLAY BALL!

Victor's commitment to the New Holland community was sometimes less obvious than his water treatment plant. On several occasions, Shaun Seymour recalls meeting with Victor in his office to solicit financial contributions for the New Holland Community Park Association. He described Victor as "gracious and generous." Mr. Seymour, an engineer at New Holland Machine Corporation, compared Victor's community support to that of New Holland Machine's President, George Delp. Both business leaders demonstrated a deep commitment to serving their community.

When the park pavilion needed to be replaced, Victor supplied the funding for a new brick structure at the western end of the park. In another situation, the park association discovered it didn't own several parcels of land in the ball diamond area. After years of use, this revelation came as a surprise. Seymour developed a different plan for making his appeal for Weaver's help. Instead of going to Weaver's office, hat in hand, he discovered a new meeting place.

Seymour learned that Victor and his brother-in-law, Ivan Martin, met occasionally at Charlie's New Holland Cut Rate Store for ice cream or milkshakes. Ivan, owner of New Holland Concrete, Inc. and Martin's Quarry, also quietly supported community projects such as the new swimming pool. Seymour planned to join the two men, buying milkshakes all around before launching into his latest park appeal. It was a successful strategy!

Victor's enjoyment of the game, and the company softball team's participation in league play there, made him an easy mark for Seymour's appeal. After identifying ownership of land parcels still needed to secure the diamond, Victor purchased the land and transferred ownership to the park association. Later, he also gave his support to the funding of a new swimming pool at the park.

On another occasion, Ivan Martin learned that a severe storm left a great amount of debris behind at the New Holland Park. He sent his men and equipment down the street from his concrete plant for a major cleanup. Neither Victor or Ivan wanted publicity for such generous actions. Mr. Seymour honored this understanding with his silence even when pressured by an enterprising reporter from *The New Holland Clarion* wanting a story—he refused to "spill the beans." The milkshakes were a good investment![22]

CHAPTER 7

Among Giants:
The Cresting Wave of the 1980s

ON THE CREST

Through the years, the Weaver company's steady pattern of growth was like a building wave. Victor made many good hiring choices to complement his own abilities. Men and women worked hard within the corporate culture to establish the Weaver brand and the reputation of integrity and quality. An industry magazine article described the Weaver organization as:

> The men who made Weaver are probably the most experienced group of specialists in poultry in general and frozen poultry in particular to sit at the head of any similar-sized company in the frozen food industry.

The group mentioned in the article included Victor Weaver, Dale Weaver, Ben Burkholder, Bill Pellman, Melvin S. Mitchell, and John Kennel. The magazine's comment was a solid endorsement of the Weaver slogan, "Nobody Knows Chicken Like the Folks at Weaver."[1]

But despite such recognition from the seventies that Weaver was an excellent company, there were signs the wave was cresting. In the past, Victor was willing to recalculate his company's direction and change course at crucial junctures. From the farmers' market beginning, to wholesale markets and, later, prepared foods, Victor willingly relinquished past successes in recognition of changing times and markets. As a leader, his gifts of entrepreneurship and vision anchored the company. But the company had never faced such a difficult decision time about its future, and the consequences seemed even greater.

When Weaver was a growing company, the pattern of yearly budgeting included hiring more staff and employees to meet the expected growth. However, sales were leveling off in the 1980s, and several years of serious financial losses raised concern.[2]

The business climate of mergers and consolidation brought new challenges. Could a regional company like Weaver survive without growing? Could it become a national contender in the big leagues? Who would lead and how could a continuing core of management surround that leadership to project the family business into a future more vastly complex than at its 1937 Sharon Hill inception? It was time to pass on the mantle of leadership and its challenges to a new generation.

In August of 1982, *Weaver Poultry Lines* announced Dale M. Weaver's election as the new president of Weaver. Victor became Chairman of the Board. Dale grew up working within the company in several capacities. He began his role as Executive Vice President in 1973 and was personally involved with many of the products developed over the years. Now taking over at the helm, he acknowledged that the burden of responsibility resting upon his shoulders had a formidable feeling. His father's shoes were rather large to fill! In the tradition of his father, Dale was committed to making decisions in consultation with his management team. He realized that growing the company would not be an easy task.

After 45 years of leadership, Victor looked forward to a more relaxing schedule than the strenuous work of the past. The following comment reflects the perseverance Victor always brought to a problem: "You have to stick through the setbacks you're in and stay with it. It's hard work. I did this all my life and stuck by it. You depend on the Lord to help you do these things."[3]

When Victor retired as chairman in 1987, Dale would also assume the role. As Victor moved towards retirement, he had the time to think of things other than business that he wanted to accomplish. The dream of a retirement community in New Holland had been taking shape in Victor Weaver's mind for several years. Shared conversations with brother-in-law, Ivan Martin, likely encouraged him to pursue his vision. On May 23, 1986, Victor made notes on a restaurant napkin enti-

In 1982, Dale Weaver became President of Weaver with Victor as Chief Executive Officer. Courtesy of New Holland Area Historical Society.

tled, "How to go about the start of a retirement home?" Perhaps he was talking that day with Ivan at Charlie's Cut Rate Store. His eight questions, written on a simple napkin, demonstrated the depth of his thinking and the lack of concrete answers to his questions.

As Victor pursued answers, he and Edith invited a small group to the Weaver home on October 13, 1987. The group included: Victor and Edith Weaver, Ivan Martin, Edward Longenecker, and Ira J. Buckwalter who met to discuss beginning a retirement community. Edward Longenecker, administrator of the Landis Homes retirement community, had never met Victor prior to this time but found him to be "quite cordial" in his presentation to the group. Although Weaver was hoping for affiliation with Landis Homes, it became apparent that continuing as separate entities was best.

Ira J. Buckwalter's October 27 letter summed up the unofficial minutes of that meeting. Their conversation had affirmed the need for such a facility in New Holland and the belief it would not be in competition with Landis Homes or the Mennonite Home. This was as far as Victor would carry his vision before his passing.

GOING NATIONAL: EXPLORING NEW TERRITORIES

Melvin Mitchell knew Dale Weaver, now president of the company, as the kid who accompanied him to market. He learned to know Dale and understand him in ways others didn't. Dale didn't have his father's easy way of relating to employees. Some thought him to be aloof, but he shared his father's vision, values and commitment to the company and its employees.

Mitchell saw Dale as a deep thinker who wrestled with the company's problems. In some respects, he believed Dale's vision was far ahead of his time with ideas of where he wanted the company to go. In the years Allon Lefever worked closely with Dale, he described Dale as a valued mentor.[4] With the question of leadership resolved, Dale Weaver took on the responsibility of leading the company from its well-established regional success into the realm of national markets—the big leagues of poultry vendors. With its New Holland base on the East Coast, "going national" presented challenges on many fronts. Other companies had networks of plants and distribution centers across the country that Weaver would have to build, but preparation on expansion had already begun before Dale became president.

In 1978, Weaver had its first poultry exhibit at a national show. The Supermarket Industry Convention and Educational Exposition gave Weaver leaders a chance to introduce the company's new marketing campaign. The goal was to become a national player in the frozen fried chicken industry. General Sales Manager, Don Welk, saw this convention as an opportunity to gain exposure with key decision makers among some of the most aggressive national retailers. Weaver underscored its own aggressiveness with their exhibit's daring new campaign slogan—"Step Aside, Southern Fried, Come on Up to Northern Fried Chicken!"[5]

Left to right: Don Herr, Don Welk, "Tank" Hutchinson of Piggly Wiggly Stores, and Dwayne Hostetter make their pitch at the national distributor/trade show. Courtesy of New Holland Area Historical Society.

Until now, the Mississippi River had been Weaver's western boundary. The convention gave company leaders an opportunity to assess retailers' interest west of the Mississippi. It also strengthened ties with their distributors far from home base in New Holland.

Despite the recession in the fiscal year 1982-83, the company moved ahead with new marketing strategies aimed at opening western outlets for their products. Weaver used three commercials to introduce its products into new market areas. Two of the commercials targeted the general public, while the third one was designed to reach corporate managers of other companies.

The company added new sales managers to oversee business in Chicago, Illinois; Columbus, Ohio; Portland, Oregon; Seattle, Washington; Washington, DC, and Dallas, Texas. A national manager would supervise these accounts. The Distribution Department

Another Weaver truck of product headed west via piggyback rail. Courtesy of New Holland Area Historical Society.

established consolidated warehouse centers serving the new areas in Chicago, Dallas and Seattle.

Weaver was encouraged by the initial response to their products from the Seattle/Portland and Dallas/Fort Worth areas. The popularity of frozen foods in these high-density, upscale neighborhood stores made them attractive markets.

The logistics of supplying such distant markets from its Pennsylvania base was a major commitment in going national. In addition to its own fleet of trucks and independent carriers, Weaver shipped products to western distribution centers in refrigerated trailers riding piggyback on flatbed railroad cars. To ensure a steady flow of product, computer telecommunications monitored warehouse inventories from the New Holland office to keep track of demand.[6]

As it moved into territories dominated by national poultry giants, the company discovered a modern version of the "Wild West" still existed. They encountered serious opposition in Texas, Arizona, the Pacific Northwest, and California. Swanson offered boneless chicken products similar to Weaver's. Banquet, Tyson and Swanson used advertising and promotions to aggressively defend their shares of the market. Their brands, already well known, set a high bar for Weaver.

In this westward expansion, Weaver abandoned its traditional "domino-effect" growth philosophy. In the past, the company used this approach to push beyond established market boundaries to include new, adjacent areas. With some spillover of Weaver brand awareness already there, it was an effective strategy of growth. Now they abandoned their domino model by skipping over large western territories in order to concentrate on the West Coast. By leaving these well-established territories far behind, they were in effect starting from scratch. They would have to educate the public to make inroads.

Melvin Mitchell acknowledged it was a new experience—more difficult and more expensive than anticipated. The cost and effects of the national campaign reverberated throughout the company and dragged down the bottom line. That sensitivity would be addressed by Keith Stuckey, a new addition to the corporate team.[7]

Keith Stuckey joined Weaver in 1982 after completing his MBA at Wharton School of Business. Ben Burkholder, part of the management team from its beginning, was transitioning towards retirement. Newer personnel like Keith and Allon Lefever illustrated how much company leadership was changing and now relying on highly-skilled and educated professionals in management. The team assembled by Victor in the early days had achieved a significant level of success and growth, but business complexities of the eighties demanded more.

Stuckey reported to President Dale Weaver. Although Stuckey had less interaction with Victor, he was impressed with Victor's concern for people and his good business instincts. Perhaps the company, with sales of approximately $150 million in the early eighties, had grown even bigger than Victor had expected. Stuckey was assigned to evaluate all aspects of Weaver's quest to become a national company. Weaver was already warehousing products as far as the West Coast. The logistics of such a commitment were indeed great. There were

Keith Stuckey joined Weaver in 1982 and began to research every aspect of the company going national. Courtesy of Keith Stuckey.

other ripple effects including the need for increased manufacturing capacity, an aggressive marketing program, and financial commitment. Declining company profitability reports reflected these increased costs.

In his early market research Stuckey learned more about the competition Weaver faced. With processing plants nationwide, Tyson Foods already had three times the sales of Weaver, and it was growing rapidly through aggressive acquisitions and sales.[8]

NEW PLANT ADDITIONS

Weaver was also looking to the South during this expansion. It purchased two facilities, one in Boaz, Alabama, and the second in Gainesville, Georgia. President Dale M. Weaver explained this action as part of Weaver's goal to increase retail and food service sales by broadening its base of product lines and adding flexibility in food-service marketing strategies.

The Eastwood Boning Company in Boaz proved to be a good investment. It employed 150 workers. Their chicken products helped Weaver accommodate the food-service market. It supplied fast food restaurants such as Wendy's, Arby's and Hardee's and brought Weaver new customers. Weaver believed the proximity to Dallas/Fort Worth and Florida markets was an added benefit.

The experience of doing business with a breeder company in North Carolina for 10 years prior to these southern additions helped Weaver gain insights about management in the South. The relationship appeared to be beneficial for both groups. One benefit to Boaz's employees was a better package of benefits from Weaver. When workers compared the benefits in their union contract with Weaver's, they eventually terminated the contract.

The Gainesville, Georgia, plant was expected to add 325,000 chickens per week to the Weaver supply. This would take some pressure off the New Holland plant already operating at full capacity. Decentralization reduced risk to the supply from a single source. The Avian Influenza experience reinforced the seriousness of such vulnerability.

However, soon there were problems with the Gainesville plant. Weaver anticipated that Gainesville production would satisfy the forecasted demand of Texas and West Coast markets. Shipping costs from the South were also cheaper. But Gainesville's volume of production was considerably less than expected, and after a few years of failure to reach its goal, Weaver had to discontinue using the plant.[9]

FOR SALE?

In this era of mergers and buyouts, other companies recognized Weaver as an attractive investment, and it began to receive unsolicited offers. In October 1983, President Dale Weaver received a personal and confidential letter from corporate acquisition and merger specialist Robert A. Weaver Jr. and Associates. Written on behalf of McCain's Foods Ltd. of Toronto, Canada, it introduced that company as "one of the leading privately held food processing companies in North America." A leader in frozen, processed foods, the McCain brand was looking for other companies to complement its holdings. Recognizing Weaver as a strong brand and market presence, led by a solid management team, the letter assured Dale that McCain's had more than a casual interest in Weaver. McCain proposed that, after acquisition, a "sound management team" would continue at Weaver. The letter ended with the specific appeal to consider selling the company to McCain.[10]

Although Dale Weaver's actual response to McCain's proposal isn't known, nothing came of the offer, but other companies' inquiries soon followed. One admirer was more persistent in its courtship. In a

1985 handwritten note on The Federal Company stationery, Lee Taylor thanked Dale and Victor for an apparent meeting he had with them. Taylor reiterated his company's desire to get better acquainted, and for the Weavers to have a greater understanding of his company. He continued:

> *If it should ever become propitious for you to consider joining with an-*
> *other company, we want you to know of our respect for and interest in*
> *you. We think we share some values in common with you and your or-*
> *ganization that are worth pursuing and preserving over the long run.*

In September of 1987, the Federal Company holding company became Holly Farms, Incorporated. Holly Farms would continue to promote the merger of the two companies. The companies were quite compatible. Holly Farms specialized in fresh poultry. Weaver had established its reputation for frozen processed chicken.[11]

Ben Burkholder is honored as the Penn-sylvania Poultry Federation Broiler In-dustry Man of 1983. Courtesy of New Holland Area Historical Society.

As Vice President of Operations, Allon Lefever was aware of all that was transpiring in the executive offices regarding the company's future. He knew Dale felt a great deal of pressure due to the resulting losses of their national campaign, and he was pondering what action to take. Should they stay the course and hope to pull through with their national aspirations, retreat to their regional status, or sell out to a larger company? When Lefever learned that Dale and board member Bill Boyle were meeting, he felt uncomfortable not knowing their agenda and what Boyle might recommend. He recognized Boyle's considerable clout and experience as the highly-respected Vice President of Marketing for the nationally-known Smucker Company.

As a close senior executive on Dale's team, Lefever was concerned enough to put his thoughts into a handwritten letter to Dale on December 26, 1985, just a few days before Dale and Boyle's meeting. Lefever wanted to counsel against a growing "sell mentality" and the reality of losing control if you sell.

He began by stating his "strong preference for working at turning this company around and moving forward rather than retracting or selling." A "survival strategy" of 12 suggested guidelines followed. He believed Weaver could survive the rough waters it was going through as a solid company with excellent brand recognition and a good management team with modern plant facilities. Weaver could be strengthened by being more selective in choosing new market areas and slow down its pace of national expansion. Even though mistakes had been made—advertising and promotion costs of going national needed to be reined in, a few expensive market campaigns in new market areas didn't do well— he was confident there could be better days ahead. Finally, he ended the letter with strong emotion: "I'd like to see this beautiful company continue as a successful enterprise into the future."

There were many aspects of this "beautiful company" Lefever felt with deep appreciation and pride. There was a positive corporate culture, a sense of trust within the strong executive team, a high-quality production line with advanced computerized machinery, and the Weavers' willingness to invest in a top-of-the-line approach for every aspect of their company. It was indeed a "beautiful company" many cherished and thought of as family.[12]

While Lefever's vision might have seemed like a daunting task, he got some unsolicited support from Bill Boyle. In his meeting with Dale, Boyle's message was—don't panic. Based on his experience with the Smucker Company, he believed Weaver could pull through its difficulties. There was more encouragement from the Smucker Company.

Boyle arranged for the senior Weaver executive team to meet with Tim and Kim Smucker. Their strategic planning team would demonstrate how Smucker did planning. Boyle's experience would be helpful to Weaver as they assessed their commitment in the national arena.[13]

As the Weaver team contemplated these voices of encouragement to their national commitment, Holly Farms joined the conversation expressing concern about the future of companies of their size.

In January of 1986, Mr. Taylor wrote a treatise of several pages to Dale Weaver. He was troubled about the future for Weaver or Holly Farms if they stood alone. He described the "giants" of the poultry industry and the "ominous threat of consolidation" facing companies like Weaver and Holly Farms. He feared the declining enforcement of antitrust laws encouraged mergers as larger companies were attempting to increase their competitive advantage.

He identified Tyson Foods and ConAgra as the two most aggressive companies big enough to "view us as prey." Taylor proposed com-

Sue Echternacht (center) and Mike Weaver of the Industrial Engineering Department's Standards and Methods staff observe Phyllis Shertz in a study of cutting techniques in the Cut-up Department.

bining forces. His company favored "decentralized operations," and "the preservation of individual identity and style of operation" for each company. The letter ended with a proposal for a confidential meeting to compare their values and possible business combination.

In the fall of 1986, a handwritten letter from Mr. Taylor ended with another appeal for Weaver to consider merging their two companies. Citing this "forbidden subject," Taylor went on to express his hope that someday he and associate Ken May could sit down with the Weavers to discuss the two companies' merger. Affirming the strengths of each company and the benefits of joining forces, he apologized for his persistence but stated, "I would be untrue to my stockholders, employees, and myself if I did not continue to try." Some events at Weaver were beginning to open the door of possibility to a more serious conversation.[14]

LOSING MONEY

The alarming financial trend at Weaver grew in 1986. The company was losing more money, and the losses grew the following year continuing into the third quarter of 1988. When sales remained flat, Weaver looked outside the company for someone with the expertise to turn things around. Melvin Mitchell, Head of Sales, now had a new boss hired from a nationally-known food company. This was a low point for Mitchell. Fortunately he stayed with the company and tried to help the new man understand Weaver's culture and markets. After a few years it became evident this new arrangement wasn't working. After Mitchell's appointment as Vice President and Chief Operations Officer, one of his first responsibilities was to let his former boss go.

Accustomed to yearly growth through most of its history, Weaver had continued to expand its workforce, but now it would have to reverse that trend. To survive, Weaver needed to become a leaner company. That decision had personal consequences for many workers and those who had to let them go.

Melvin Mitchell would have to carry out orders to let people go. Victor believed it was important that every worker feel important and respected. Like Victor, Mitchell developed relationships with many employees. He even accompanied a chicken-catching crew on their job at 3 o'clock one morning. Now it was his difficult task to give them notice—their jobs at Weaver were over. As he listened to their concerns, and the impact that loss of employment would have on them and their families, he shared their disappointment. This was hard work.[15]

Supervisor Mike Good, who began working at Weaver in the seventies, believed Weaver's difficulties began when it stepped beyond its boundaries as a successful regional company in its efforts to become a national player. One of the added expenses of this effort was hiring the "big guns" from national companies to direct this effort. Their salaries, and other costs, made the company "top heavy," adding to the financial stresses already happening.

There were several factors at work contributing to the financial decline. The Gainesville plant's problems had financial repercussions. Poultry prices were depressed throughout the industry. Reduced sales of prepared nuggets to a major food-service customer also had an impact. Although the volume of fresh chicken sales increased, there was less profit in this.

In addition, many companies were expanding their frozen food lines. This intensified competition for the limited display space in supermarket freezer cases. Additional administrative costs in 1986 reflected increased staffing to support Weaver's national expansion plans. By January of 1988, administrative and general expenses were being cut back by reducing staff, advertising, promotions and market research.[16]

Adding to its problems, Weaver was being challenged on its home turf by Tyson Foods. Weaver had a commanding 60% market share in the Northeast quadrant of the country. As Weaver took the offensive by expanding into western markets where Tyson was dominant, Tyson's response put Weaver on the defensive in the Northeast. An example of Tyson's pitch to supermarkets was very attractive—buy one trailer of product and get a second one free. Weaver was also losing display space

The "Step Aside Southern Fried" campaign went well in the Northeast, but got a cool reception in southern states. Courtesy of New Holland Area Historical Society.

in these supermarkets to this new rival. But the campaign went beyond merchandise. A Tyson ad on Boston billboards challenged Weaver's popular Rondelet chicken breast patty. Its challenge was that Tyson had breast meat in its patties, what does Weaver have? Weaver was feeling the heat with higher costs than expected in its offensive west of the Mississippi River and now fighting a defensive battle in the Northeast.

Holly Farms intensified its appeal to Weaver by unveiling their Strategic Plan. This was the solution to their problems. Holly had successfully resisted a Tyson take-over attempt but believed it needed better defenses. To counter Tyson's aggressive juggernaut of acquisition, Holly proposed a merger with Weaver. Holly Farms was also expanding into processed beef products. They were convinced this new company would be too big for Tyson to pursue. An investment banker hired to assess the plan agreed with Holly Farms: It was doubtful that Tyson would dare take on this new, larger Holly Farms.[17]

HOLLY FARMS RENEWS ITS MERGER PROPOSAL

During the summer of 1987, Weaver was ready to seriously consider Holly Farms' proposal. Holly's assurance through the Strategic Plan that a Tyson take-over would be unlikely must have been very encouraging to Weaver. Weaver management's ability to run the company with minimal Holly supervision was also appealing. Conversation between the companies continued to a conclusion in 1988.

As Weaver considered the merger with Holly Farms, Keith Stuckey became more involved in the procedures. He succeeded John Kennel as Corporate Secretary and did most of the negotiating work with attorneys. Dale and Victor gave him specific ground rules for Weaver's goals. Even though the two companies were a good fit for each other, Weaver wanted to retain as much independence of operation as possible, and they wanted the Weaver brand to continue. Their wishes were granted in the final agreement.[18]

On January 29, 1988, a front-page story in the *Lancaster New Era* heralded the news that Holly Farms Corporation had reached an "understanding" to acquire Victor F. Weaver, Inc. Weaver responded that a deal hadn't been finalized. Pondering the uncertainty of Weaver's future, the decision came with reluctance a few months later at a stockholders' meeting.

REWARDING LONG-TERM EMPLOYEES

Just prior to finalizing the sale to Holly Farms, the Weavers decided to share some of their own stock with employees who helped the company achieve its success over the years. This was a significant gift for employees; it was a gracious act. Grateful employees sent many notes of thanks and letters of appreciation to

HOLLY FARMS FOODS, INC.
1203 School Street, P.O. Box 88, Wilkesboro, North Carolina 28697-0088
(919) 838-2171

RECEIVED MAY 2 3 1988

May 19, 1988

KENNETH N. MAY, PH.D.
CHAIRMAN AND
CHIEF EXECUTIVE OFFICER

Mr. Victor F. Weaver
Chairman Emeritus
Victor F. Weaver, Inc.
P. O. Box 1156
New Holland, PA 17557-0901

Dear Victor:

I was extremely pleased and impressed to learn that we have 118 new shareholders in Holly Farms Corporation due to your generosity and appreciation for the efforts of all of the employees of Victor F. Weaver, Inc. It has been my observation that, although many people talk about their concern and esteem for their employees and coworkers, few are willing to make personal sacrifices to help others.

This gesture further strengthens my convictions that Victor F. Weaver, Inc. is an organization that will have a very strong and viable future as a member of the Holly Farms Corporation team. I am sure that all of the employees will never forget the founder of their very fine company and his concern for their well-being.

It is a real pleasure to be associated with you, Dale and the other fine people at Victor F. Weaver, Inc.

Best personal regards,

Sincerely yours,

Ken

Kenneth N. May, Ph.D.

KNM/jd

cc: Dale Weaver
     Lee Taylor

Ken May's letter to Victor praising stock of the Weaver family given to employees before the sale to Holly Farms. Courtesy of the Newswanger family.

the Weaver family for their generosity and good fortune! Others were also impressed.

In a May 19, 1988, letter addressed to Victor F. Weaver, Chairman Emeritus, Holly Farms Chair and CEO, Kenneth N. May, praised this unusual generosity given to 118 new shareholders observing that, "although many people talk about their concern and esteem for their employees and coworkers, few are willing to make the personal sacrifices to help others.... I am sure that all of the employees will never forget the founder of their very fine company and his concern for their well-being."[19]

STOCKHOLDERS' MEETING AT YODER'S

Weaver stockholders met at Yoder's Steak House and Restaurant in New Holland on April 25, 1988. They reluctantly faced the reality of Holly's proposal in the form of a thick binder of merger information. It summarized factors contributing to Weaver's financial situation and the specifics of the merger. In the introductory pages of the proposal, Chairman of the Board of Directors and President, Dale Weaver, noted the Board of Directors' careful consideration of this merger as "fair, and in the best interests of Weavers' shareholders." The Weaver Board of Directors recommended that shareholders vote in favor of the proposal, and with their consent, the deed was soon done. The company Victor and Edith birthed in 1937 was no longer theirs, the mantle had passed to others beyond the family.[20]

Janet Newswanger recalled a phone call from her father. It wasn't his custom to call just to chat, and his message this time was out of the ordinary. The company was sold in a merger with Holly Farms. The decision gave rise to mixed emotions: sadness and relief. For Victor and Dale, resignation was perhaps the most pronounced feeling. Even though it appeared to be the best solution possible in those circumstances, the family mourned this loss. The company was passing beyond the family's control.[21]

Looking back in hindsight, despite all the positive support for Weaver's decision to go national, that decision appeared to be the company's biggest misstep. Allon Lefever believed Tyson Foods' serious challenge to Weaver's turf in the Northeast was the final blow. Without that Tyson offensive, Weaver might have been able to survive.

Keith Stuckey believed going national was an opportunity that might have been achievable if the pace of expansion had been slowed and the markets chosen had been most amenable to newcomers. Action in some markets like Texas and the West Coast might have been delayed. He saw them as the toughest markets to crack and the most expensive due to the distance from home base and the expense of aggressive marketing.

Although the company could have continued in this fashion for several more years, Stuckey was skeptical the momentum of merger and consolidation forces could be resisted successfully in the long run.[22]

According to Michael Mitchell, family business consultant at Elizabethtown College's High Center, the Weavers' family business experience wasn't unusual. Many families find it difficult to pass on their business to succeeding generations. Thirty percent of family businesses make it into the second generation and fifteen percent to the third. But by the fourth generation, only four percent percent survive.[23]

Such cold statistics are of little comfort for families who have worked hard to grow their enterprises only to see them fade away or pass to others. The Weaver identity didn't disappear completely. The personal relationship forged with the Holly management team in conversations and correspondence over several years was some consolation. It was also comforting to know their companies shared similar values. Another consolation might have been that in all their years of business, the Weavers were able to allay the fears of some in the church. Success in business had not undermined their identity or faith.

THE STEWARDSHIP OF TALENTS: A FAITHFUL EXAMPLE

When the Weavers began their venture in the 1930s, many Mennonites perceived the business world in a shadow of suspicion that wouldn't fade away for decades to come. They feared business values would erode their agrarian traditions and church teachings as some strayed beyond such boundaries. *Gelassenheit*, or submission to Christ and His community, was the model of humility for all to follow. Many in the Mennonite Church considered the individualism of commerce and the profit motive to be a corrupting influence on all who ventured into this realm.

Roy S. Burkholder's book title expressed the concern for Mennonites entering the world of business. *Courtesy of Roy S. Burkholder.*

In his history of the Weaverland Mennonite Church, Roy S. Burkholder held up two congregational members, Victor F. Weaver and Ivan M. Martin, as entrepreneurs who had successfully negotiated the challenges of the business world. The complexity of their situations and the accumulating wealth sometimes made it difficult for them to relate in a brotherhood where topics of conversation included crop yields, the price of tobacco and other crops, or vagaries of the weather.

Burkholder sums up his observations: Victor's life was a model of humility and integrity. He was never comfortable at the center of attention and preferred to do his "good works" in anonymity. His frequently voiced motto "Beware when all men speak well of you," succinctly encapsulated a caution that guided him. Described as "shy, retiring, but always compassionate," Victor's personality was well suited to not thinking more highly of himself because of what he had achieved.[24]

Whether in business dealings or relating to his neighbor, Victor lived by his faith principles. He would rather go the second mile in a disagreement, even risk being taken advantage of, rather than defend his own point of view. A neighbor's repeated complaint was a test for Victor. The neighbor believed that a surveyor's pin placement incorrectly divided the two properties. After several encounters, Victor's response finally resolved the problem—"Here's the pin," he said, "put it where you want it and I'll be satisfied." The neighbor walked away, and the subject never came up again.

Although Victor was committed to the church, as a successful businessperson he felt his wealth influenced some to elevate him above others in the congregation. Even the family's modest lifestyle didn't keep some from perceiving them differently. Preachers warned about the dangers of accumulated wealth. Church periodical articles criticized the greed of the capitalist system. But wealthy congregants often found themselves among the first to be asked to contribute when the church had a need. Victor's response was always gracious and generous.[25]

HOLLY FARMS: THE NEW COMPANY

Holly Farms trusted Weaver to continue managing the company and kept their promise of minimal interference. Downsizing changes already begun prior to the merger were turning the company around. It was more profitable and in better shape even before the merger was concluded. In the new arrangement, Weaver used some of its discretionary freedom to improve its situation. Don Welk was one of the people helping to turn the company around financially. Changes in the marketing department and staff cuts made Weaver less top-heavy.

Every month Dale Weaver and Melvin Mitchell traveled to the Holly Farms corporate headquarters in North Carolina to give their reports. Although now part of Holly Farms, Weaver's brand and quality products made it an attractive entity to others. In its peak years, Weaver enjoyed a remarkable sixty percent share of the Northeast market. Larger companies would find it cheaper to buy their way into this market area instead of building their own organization. Weaver was now part of a public company with Holly Farms' stock available on the open market. It wasn't long until the "poultry giants" Holly Farms' Lee Taylor had described to Victor took notice and were on the move.[26]

DANCE OF THE GIANTS: TYSON FOODS AND CONAGRA

In the spring of 1989, the struggle between Tyson Foods and ConAgra began for control of Holly Farms. Holly Farms' hope that its company was too big to be a target of acquisition had failed. It also tried to resist a hostile take-over with an arrangement known as a "crown jewel lockup." In such a situation, Holly Farms would sell to a designated company deemed most desirable to management. If such an action became necessary, Holly Farms favored acquisition by ConAgra, but Tyson Foods successfully challenged the crown jewel lockup provision in a Delaware court. Now the highest bidder could win control of Holly Farms.

The bidding for Holly Farms' stock opened at $49 per share and continued to escalate until the board of directors couldn't refuse Tyson's grand $70 per share offer. The board dissolved the crown jewel lockup and accepted the $1.4 billion dollar agreement. ConAgra was compensated for its consent to drop out of the action, and all litigation between the two firms ended. The Delaware Chancery Court presided over the three companies' transactions. Holly Farms and Weaver now belonged to Tyson Foods. With Tyson processing more than 16.5 million chickens a week, far more output than Holly and Weaver, they were now indeed among the poultry giants!

Weaver employees who received stock from the family before sale to Holly Farms, now had a second windfall. The value of Holly Farms' stock had appreciated substantially as the two giants struggled for control. It's ironic that the Weaver family, who preferred their company's relationship with Holly Farms, also profited significantly from their holdings in the Tyson take-over.[27]

Michael Good began hanging chickens on the line for $2.00 per hour in 1972. He rose to supervisory positions at Weaver and Holly Farms and later became Tyson's Complex Manager at New Holland. Courtesy of Michael Good.

Michael Good had seen all the changes. He continued to work at the New Holland plant through all its changes in ownership. Given its circumstances, he believed Weaver's sale to Holly Farms was a good move at that time. This arrangement worked well. However, Weaver was now part of a company with its stock publicly available and vulnerable to market forces. When the bidding war between Tyson Foods and ConAgra ended with the hostile take-over of Holly Farms, many aspects of the Weaver company, including its corporate identity, faded away. As part of Tyson Foods, it no longer operated as it had with Holly Farms, a semi-independent company.

Now the Weaver plant's main function was to process chickens. There was no need for its own departments such as research and development, marketing, or others. Business-related decisions were now made elsewhere in the Tyson organization. The "beautiful company" of the past was now only a memory.[28]

THE FOUNDERS' PASSING

Till the end of his life, Victor was concerned about others' welfare. Albert Kunkle spent the last 15 of his 30 years at Weaver as Customer Service Manager. Although he lost his job when Tyson Foods took over, the severance package was "quite good." Kunkle enjoyed his years at Weaver and, as others have mentioned, the company felt like family to him. Even with its steady growth, Albert felt the family feeling continued because, "as it got bigger the Weaver family was still able to keep its values."

Victor and Edith, partners in life and business. Courtesy of the Newswanger family.

Kunkle said that Victor's personal connections with employees gave them a feeling of belonging. With genuine interest, he sat in the lunchroom and chatted with employees about their families or other topics not related to their work.

One day while Victor was standing on the loading dock, Albert asked him what he believed to be his greatest achievement. By the late 1970s, the company was in its peak years. Without hesitation, Victor replied that all the jobs Weaver was providing for families gave him the most satisfaction.

The last time Albert Kunkle saw Victor, he was in the Lancaster General Hospital. Victor's battle with cancer was nearing its end. Before his visit, Albert determined not to talk about business, but wanted to simply relate as a brother in the faith. He was barely through the door of the hospital room before Victor greeted him, asking, "Do you still have a job?" Albert was glad he could answer yes, he still had a job; at that point Tyson Foods had not yet let workers go. They talked shop a bit then moved on to other things, but it struck Kunkle how, in those circumstances, Victor's first concern was for his visitor.

After a remarkable journey from humble beginnings, Victor and Edith successfully built their company and served it well. Leaving the company in others' hands, Victor retired in 1987. He passed away on November 8, 1989. He died at home after his seven-month struggle with cancer. He was 76.

Later, Ben Burkholder, of the Weaver executive team and member of the same church congregation as Kunkle, demonstrated this same caring spirit. By this time, Tyson had ended Albert's employment. Ben told him, "If you ever need anything, let me know." It was part of the family spirit demonstrated at Weaver. It would have made Victor proud![29]

Years later at age 83, Edith Weaver was looking back on her life. She shared early memories of their company and family history with Ruth McDaniel, newly married to grandson Kendall Newswanger. She recalled butchering those first chickens for Sharon Hill Market. Some of the chickens had to be hung from a tree at their Blue Ball farmhouse. Edith spoke with energy as she recalled the good old days. It had been a good, meaningful life. She believed the company's end was a "good thing" because she said "the weight" was gone. Edith was happy as she remembered that past. Together she and Victor had accomplished much.[30]

When Edith passed away on April 23, 2005, her grandchildren's remarks at the funeral captured some of her spirit. Greg Newswanger remembered his grandmother's hands that prepared meals for family and visitors, helped with the work of the church, and paid grocery bills including the grandchildren's favorite shopping choices. Her model of generosity and stewardship was noteworthy. Both Greg and his brother, Randy, remember Edith's sense of humor and how her giggle could grow "from a chuckle into a crescendo" of mirth that drew others in.[31]

THE DREAM OF GARDEN SPOT VILLAGE BEGUN ON A RESTAURANT NAPKIN

Victor's passing left his son Dale to complete his father's vision of a New Holland retirement center. As Dale gave leadership to the plans taking shape, the proposals drew community opposition, a clash of values, and personal attacks. Some expressed concern for the traditional preservation of Lancaster County's productive farmland. The encroachment of such a venture, ironically to be known as Garden Spot Village, appeared to threaten that very "garden spot" revered and promoted with Lancaster County pride. Preservationists lamented loss of the land and resentment that people of wealth could override agricultural tradition to justify this enterprise.

Town meetings with Earl Township supervisors became increasingly heated. Emotions peaked when the rumor of an alleged death threat appeared in the *Lancaster New Era* newspaper. At the next town hall meeting, security measures included the personal search of all those entering the hall, and plain clothes officers in the

Victor's questions written on a restaurant napkin became a visual reminder to Dale, after his father's passing, of his new responsibility to complete the task. Courtesy of Garden Spot Village archives.

audience. Word of these attempts to cool things down only added fuel to the fire.[32]

Martin Weaver, Dale's uncle and a supporter of the retirement center, confided in a neighbor the morning after this meeting, saying Dale had come "this close"—gesturing with a small gap between thumb and forefinger—to dropping the whole affair. But, Martin said, "We talked him out of it." It took courage for Dale and others to continue.[33]

While many still had good words to say about Victor, Dale bore the brunt of negative criticism for this venture. He emphasized his father's intentions: Victor saw the work of establishing a retirement center in New Holland as a way of giving back to the community he valued and that had helped him to become successful.

Much of the opposition seemed to subside with abandonment of the Eberly farm as the building site, in favor of the Ranck farm closer to town. This location made more sense with its contiguous location to New Holland Borough. Today Garden Spot Village has a reputation of excellence. Owned and operated as a nonprofit organization, it reflects the values and a degree of community commitment less likely if part of a national chain.

Steve Lindsey, Chief Executive Officer of Garden Spot Village, believes that Victor wanted to serve the needs of residents and the surrounding community. Lindsey said Garden Spot was intended to

Garden Spot Village became a reality as son Dale took up the task. Courtesy of Garden Spot Village.

be part of the community, not an island unto itself. Residents have the opportunity to contribute unspent monthly meal funds for others through the Food Bank and Crossnet Ministries. This is one example of support for local needs. Residents have also supported international projects as a way to reach out beyond their own community.

More than half of the village's present 1,000 residents are from outside Lancaster County, and they bring a significant amount of financial and other resources to the community. Local businesses benefit from this infusion of people and finances. Garden Spot is a major employer of many in surrounding communities.

Another recent local initiative, the Cooperative Living House Project, developed without government funding, provides affordable housing for those unable to afford living at Garden Spot. These residents contribute thirty percent of their monthly income to live in the cooperative house. Each bedroom has its own bathroom. The general design of the house is similar to the Weavers' Sarasota, Florida, home they planned to share with friends. The rooms surround a center commons area of communal living space that includes dining and kitchen facilities. For most, it is a welcome alternative to living alone or in other difficult circumstances.[34]

South Custer Avenue in New Holland as it appears today. Author's photo.

Several years ago, a Victor F. Weaver, Inc. exhibit at the New Holland Area Historical Society displayed the company's historical development. It did not include anything about the retirement center. Although the exhibit received many favorable reviews, one visiting Garden Spot resident expressed indignation through an anonymous letter. The letter castigated those in charge of the display for their failure to recognize, in the writer's opinion, Garden Spot Village as Victor's crowning achievement. It was a novel validation of Victor's vision.[35]

———————————

Today, a visit to South Custer Avenue reveals no vestiges of the early Weaver days as seen in the painting below. The houses, garden plot, and early outbuildings have all given way to the expanding Weaver, and now Tyson plant. It is a visual reminder of the dynamics of change—the positive growth of their business eventually pushed the Weavers from this site and ownership of their company. But the Weaver brand, a remnant of the past, still exists as part of Tyson Foods. The community and others continue to benefit from the family's generosity.

The Weaver place on South Custer Avenue much as it was after the move from the Blue Ball farm. Art by Glen Eshleman. Courtesy of the Newswanger family.

CHAPTER 8

Legacy

Victor Weaver would be uncomfortable with the attention given to him at this writing, but it is important from the perspective of history to remember and reflect. His life still speaks to us of his simple faith, humble spirit, and his genuine caring for others that demonstrate the inner moorings guiding his life. Beyond the physical reminders of Victor's success, his legacy is the enduring testimony of his faith commitment in the midst of everyday life as a Christian and a businessman.

Victor's legacy can be considered in three specific dimensions: entrepreneurship, giving, and faith and family.

ENTREPRENEURSHIP

Victor Weaver was an unassuming man who, along with his wife, Edith, began with a simple market stand in a suburban Philadelphia neighborhood. He soon saw the potential for the growth of his business. His awakening entrepreneurial spirit would serve him well over the next 40 years. Victor relied on his own intuition more than careful analysis as he built his business. He was a good judge of character and some of his early hires grew with him and the company to become an integral part of his management team and corporate culture for many years.

Victor was one to look ahead. His fascination with new things included a curiosity about the changing scene in business. At critical times, he chose to abandon past successes to guide his company in new directions. Victor's progressive outlook in business kept him looking ahead for better ways of doing things, developing new products, and using the best equipment. When he was building his Camp Hebron cottage, he used state-of-the-art materials which proved to be a good investment over many years to the present day. Victor had the same outlook when it came to spending money on his business.

Victor has been described as a "brilliant strategic guy," with an inherent, God-given ability impossible to acquire. Victor was always steps ahead of others but he also demonstrated perseverance. The failure of a product in 1946 didn't keep him from trying again in the sixties in what became Weaver's greatest achievement. Sometimes Victor had to wait for the public to catch up with his vision and for changes in technology.[1]

At the heart of this story is a man with a keen sense of business who created a company in the small-town atmosphere of New Holland, Pennsylvania, with its closely held values and work ethic. Former employees who gathered at the New Holland Area Historical Society's exhibit of Victor F. Weaver, Inc. were nostalgic. They remembered what it was like to be part of this company. Bill Pellman and Dwayne Hostetter, who worked in sales, reminisced. Hostetter noted that the camaraderie among employees was the best part of his job. Pellman remembered Victor's entrepreneurship and ability to

Mary Lou Weaver remembers the past at the New Holland Area Historical Society's exhibit of Victor F. Weaver, Inc. Courtesy of New Holland Area Historical Society.

look ahead, guiding his company in a highly competitive business. Mary Lou Weaver, not a relative of Victor, expressed some of the loss others likely felt. She observed, "It was a wonderful company and we were like a family."[2]

The proud motto, "Nobody Knows Chicken Like the Folks at Weaver," had a folksy, down-home appeal, the neighborliness of small-town American entrepreneurship. More than a slogan, however, it was the trademark for a progressive, family-owned business with many innovations and a commitment to quality products.

Many in the poultry industry recognized the innovations of the Weavers. A front-page newspaper headline in 1986 proclaimed, "The Man: Modest Victor Weaver Is a Giant in the Poultry Business." In the article, Mel Mitchell credits Victor and Dale's ability to look ahead and to see the opportunities that often led to Weaver innovations. While Victor was a visionary who others saw as "way ahead of the industry," Paul Martin recognized that his entrepreneurship succeeded in part due to hard work and his determination to solve problems.

Some of the company's innovations were:

- Weaver's environmentally-controlled broiler houses changed the nature of the local industry.

- One of the first to offer cut-up chicken to consumers and take his company in that direction.

- Frozen breaded fried chicken was among its most notable pioneering efforts that introduced a new prepared food product to the frozen food industry.

- The Weaver Chicken Roll was a catalyst for Weaver's entry into the prepared foods market. Chicken Franks became popular as Americans became concerned about diet.[3]

- Victor was also described as both the "originator and popularizer" of frozen breaded fried chicken. In the sixties, Weaver's success with this product soon had larger companies enthusiastically following his lead.[4]

Perhaps some of the nostalgia former Weaver employees felt included mourning the trend of business consolidation and merger, the bigness and homogenization coming to small-town America. Yet, some of the memories were also a recognition of the initiative and resourcefulness of small, family enterprises where success brought employment and other benefits to the surrounding communities.

Former Weaver executive and entrepreneur, Allon Lefever, summarized this sentiment well in his writing:

There is a special beauty in the smaller, community-focused family businesses and the successful entrepreneurs who have a personal relationship with their associates…entrepreneurs have a unique opportunity to form value-driven companies. The importance of values and culture in guiding your business and personal life cannot be underestimated.[5]

GIVING AND SERVICE

The word philanthropy seems too formal, too institutional, when describing Victor and Edith's giving. In their lifetime, they gave financial support to others through many causes but the word philanthropy wasn't likely a word they would have used to describe giving.

Giving was a natural response to the needs of the church and other organizations. Their long-term commitments were at times sacrificial in the sense that they were made with the anticipation of future business income. At that time there was no foundation or board of directors giving out of a significant amount of wealth accrued. In consultation with Edith, they simply gave. After their discussions and decisions were made, it was always Edith who wrote out and signed the checks!

Victor's life work included a variety of service involvements in his church and community. Although he was heavily invested in managing his company, his vision went beyond its bottom line. Board memberships came with financial expectations, but as he moved beyond the familiarity of his corporate role, he found opportunities for personal growth.

Victor's long-term commitment to Philhaven has been well established. There was a mutual benefit in serving on the board all those years. While Victor may not have been able to articulate this, family members clearly saw that in Victor's life it gave him a sense of place—belonging with others committed to a greater cause.

When he opened his doors to Puerto Rican workers, Victor's concern for them went beyond filling slots on the processing lines. He gave many an opportunity to begin a new life here. He invited them to take advantage of opportunities for promotion within the company in ways that benefitted both employer and employees. He took an interest in their lives and families, and invited them into his home for coffee and talks about faith. He supported the establishment of the Spanish Mennonite Church in New Holland with his time and money.

He hired people of color in management positions such as the Human Resource Department, well before this was the norm. Weaver offered classes to learn English and mainland culture. Some pages of the company newsletter communicated promotion opportunities in Spanish with the message that all were invited to consider greater opportunities at Weaver. Not everyone stayed with Weaver all their working lives. For some it was a stepping stone to workplaces and experiences beyond New Holland. Many, like Francisco Delgado Jr., settled into and became important members of their communities.

The United Service Foundation, Inc. board of directors, left to right. Front row: Greg Newswanger, Juji Woodring, Dawn Isley, Irene Martin Weaver, Olivia Mc-Daniel. Second row: Dan Hess, consultant, Avin Newswanger, Janet Newswanger, Larry Newswanger, Randy Newswanger, Kendall Newswanger, Ruth McDaniel, Geoff Isley, Ursa Woodring. 4th generation not board members: Olivia McDaniel, Avin Newswanger, Ursa Woodring. Courtesy of the Newswanger family.

The United Service Foundation, Inc. was one of the ways the Weaver family continued to give to others beyond their lifetime. The family foundation was established in 1969 with: Victor and Edith, Irene and Dale Weaver, and Janet and Larry Newswanger as directors. Presently, grandchildren also serve on the board.

The foundation began with small grants to local nonprofits. After Tyson bought Holly Farms, the foundation had the ability to significantly increase its giving to offset taxes from the sale of Holly stock. A foundation brochure includes the following mission statement:

> The United Service Foundation, rooted in the Anabaptist Christian tradition, seeks to grow the Kingdom of God by building and facilitating strong families and communities that practice love, learning, forgiveness and justice.

In a foundation board meeting at Camp Hebron, family members reminisced about Victor's life. Near the end of the meeting,

The Weaver Family from left to right: Dale Weaver, Irene Martin Weaver, Kendall Newswanger, Janet Weaver Newswanger, Larry Newswanger. Second row: Sue Ann Weaver, Dawn Weaver, Victor Weaver, Edith Weaver, Tina Weaver, Greg Newswanger, Randy Newswanger. Courtesy of the Newswanger family.

daughter Janet said of her father, "We are doing what he wanted to do in retirement." Through the foundation, they are carrying out the work he looked forward to doing.[6]

In 2019, the family celebrated the fiftieth year of the foundation. The 2016 annual report shows the United Service Foundation, Inc. gave over $500,000 to over 40 church and community organizations and educational institutions.

FAITH AND FAMILY

Victor's commitment to his faith and family was elemental. With his brother, Raymond, he researched their family's lineage with an awareness of their ancestral origins. His Mennonite heritage influenced his commitment to the church. It was an overshadowing dynamic shaping him.

In some respects, Victor wasn't a complicated man—his business philosophy emanated from his Christian faith. His values were well known even to company truck drivers whom Victor asked to keep "the Sabbath" by not starting their engines until 12:01 Monday morning.

For Victor, the hierarchy of employee specialization didn't change an individual employee's importance. Often more than in spoken words, his personal interaction and caring personality demonstrated his convictions. It was an example caught more than taught within his management circle by others who practiced similar involvement with employees.

Delbert Seitz saw Victor as "a genuine Christian businessman who wanted to use his abilities to serve God and people. He was about as saintly a businessman as I ever worked for. He genuinely cared about people without ulterior motives." Another contemporary business person said Victor was "a good businessman." He paused and then clarified—"a good Mennonite businessman." He concluded that the Weaver company wasn't a Christian business, but a business operated by Christians.[7]

Many more testimonials regarding Victor's business ethics and faith values could be cited from industry leaders and others of various persuasions. Speaking to a reporter, Dale shared his perspective of the family's commitment:

> ...we take our Christian commitment seriously, we believe that when you love the Lord and serve him, that is the first commandment. Then you treat others as you want to be treated yourself. This is the driving force of the Weaver family.[8]

Finally, it is only fitting for Victor to have the last word and, while it is characteristically brief, it states the bedrock of his faith and action. It comes from a response written to a question asked many years ago. The origin of the question and its context aren't clear, but his answer leaves no doubt.

"Can a Christian be a businessman?"

A businessman sure can, but he cannot do it by himself. He needs the help of God through Christ and the encouragement of his wife and family. Working with people near you and in the community in which you live gives a personal satisfaction. It is also a pleasant experience to see your community grow along with the business in which you are involved. This all takes hard work, and the goal must be to live for others and be a servant of man and not the ruler. I am thankful to God for what he has done for me. I trust that your experience may be the same in Christ Jesus and praise the Lord for what he has done for you or can do for you.

Endnotes

CHAPTER 1: VICTOR AND EDITH WEAVER

1. Martin G. Weaver, *Mennonites of Lancaster Conference* (Scottdale, Pa.: Mennonite Publishing House, 1931), 122-123; Martin G. Weaver, *Weaverland Settlement, Settlers Graveyard and Its Four Plantations Now Divided into 45 Farms* (New Holland, Pa.: Martin G. Weaver, 1933), 27-32; Raymond H. Weaver and Victor F. Weaver, *Descendents of Francis B. Weaver* (June 1981), 2.

2. Weaver, *Mennonites,* 122; Weaver, *Descendents,* 2-4.

3. Weaver, *Weaverland,* 32.

4. Weaver, *Descendants,* 1.

5. Weaver, *Descendants,* 5.

6. Martin H. & Vera B. Weaver, and Glori Brubaker, *A Collection of Stories from the Life of Martin H. Weaver* (Lititz, Pa.: 2004), 20-21; Interview with Lamar Weaver, March 25, 2020.

7. Weaver, *A Collection,* 21-22; Interview with Merle Good, December 26, 2019.

8. Weaver, *A Collection,* 12-14, 18.

9. Roy S. Burkholder, *Be Not Conformed To This World: A Narrative History of the Weaverland Mennonites, 1900-1975* (Morgantown, PA: Masthof Press, 1998 reprint), 170, 176-177. Don Jacobs counseled not to forget the influence of these sisters in that era as they took an unusually active role in their husbands' businesses.

10. Family Reflections at Camp Hebron, July 4, 2017.

11. Ibid.

12. Ibid.

13. Interview with Merle Good, December 26, 2019.

14. Family Reflections, July 4, 2017; Interview with Larry and Janet Newswanger, March 21, 2020.

CHAPTER 2: BIRTH OF A BUSINESS: THE MARKET ERA, 1937-1950s

1. *The First Forty Years: A History of Victor F. Weaver, Inc.*, January 1978, Publication No. 118, 4.

2. Benjamin L. Burkholder, *The Weaver Story,* Unpublished, 3.

3. Ibid.

4. Interview with Lamar S. Weaver, January 24, 2018.

5. *The First Forty Years,* 4-5.

6. Burkholder, *The Weaver Story*, 1-2.

7. Ibid., 4.

8. Ibid., 1.

9. Ibid., 2-7.

10. Ibid., 6-7.

11. *The First Forty Years,* 6.

12. Donald Welk, "History of Victor F. Weaver, Inc. as Presented at the Management Dinner Meeting," March 25, 1977, 3.

13. Interview with Melvin Mitchell, April 25, 2017; Interview with Larry Newswanger, October 6, 2017.

14. Interview with Melvin Mitchell, April 25, 2017.

15. Interview with Melvin Mitchell, May 16, 2017.

16. *The First Forty Years,* 6-7; Burkholder, *The Weaver Story*, 7-8.

17. Burkholder, *The Weaver Story*, 8.

CHAPTER 3: PHILHAVEN HOSPITAL: A LIFE-LONG SERVICE COMMITMENT

1. Louise Stoltzfus, *As Long As the Grass Grows and Water Flows: The Story of Philhaven* (Mt. Gretna, Pa.: Philhaven, 2002), 4-6.

2. Ibid., 2-6.

3. Albert Q. Maisel, "Bedlam 1946: Most U.S. Mental Hospitals Are a Shame and a Disgrace," *Life Magazine*, May 6, 1946, 102-109.

4.   Stoltzfus, 7-8.

5.   Maisel, 115-117.

6.   Ibid., 118.

7.   Ibid., 119.

8.   Stoltzfus, 11-16.

9.   Stoltzfus, 10-12, 14.

10.   Interview with Larry Newswanger, April 24, 2019.

11.   Melvin Wert, "Personal Reflections." Received by Allan W. Shirk, December 14, 2016.

12.   Philhaven Hospital Board Minutes, February 9, 1949.

13.   Philhaven Hospital Board Minutes, February 19, 1971.

14.   Stoltzfus, 61-62.

15.   S. Dale High, Phone conversation, October 11, 2016.

16.   Interview with Irene M. Weaver, March 2, 2018; Interview with Larry and Janet Newswanger, April 24, 2019.

CHAPTER 4: CHANGING DIRECTION: THE WHOLESALE MARKET, 1950-1960s

1.   *The First Forty Years: A History of Victor F. Weaver, Inc.,* January, 1978, 7-8.

2.   Interview with William Pellman, November 29, 2016.

3.   *The First Forty Years,* 7.

4.   "The Million Mile Man," *Weaver Poultry Lines,* July 1979, 3; Interview with Lee Weaver, January 21, 2020.

5.   "Truck Graphics Catch Safety Award," *Weaver Poultry Lines*, 28 Oct. 1982, 2.

6.   *The First Forty Years,* 8-9; Interviews with Lamar Weaver, January 24, 2018; March 25, 2020.

7.   Interview with Jesse Yoder, March 24, 2018.

8.   Interviews with Allon Lefever, April 22, 2020; April 19, 2020.

9.   "The Broiler Tradition, a Family," *Entree,* March-April 1990; Interview with Robert Sr. and Lois Brubaker, June 11, 2020.

10.   Interview with Larry Newswanger, February 21, 2020.

11. Family Reflections at Camp Hebron, July 4, 2017.

12. James Martin, "Serving at Camp Hebron." Received Sept. 8, 2020; phone conversation, Sept. 9, 2020

13. Melvin Wert, "Personal Story." Received by Allan W. Shirk, November 29, 2016.

14. Interviews with Larry Newswanger, December 20, 2019; June 8, 2020.

CHAPTER 5: THE PUERTO RICO CONNECTION

1. Joel Horst Nofziger, Ramona Rivera Santiago, and Joanne Hess Siegrist, "An Introduction to the Hispanic Mennonites of Lancaster County: Origins and Early Years," *Pennsylvania Mennonite Heritage* 38, no. 1 (2015) 2.

2. Ibid., 7-8.

3. Ibid., 13; Interview with Lester Blank, April 3, 2020.

4. Lester Blank, "William Lauver." Received by Allan W. Shirk, April 3, 2020.

5. Roy S. Burkholder, *Be Not Conformed,* 181-182.

6. Horst, Santiago and Siegrist, "Introduction," 12-13.

7. Ibid., 9.

8. Tina Hess Glanzer, "Personal Story." Received by Allan W. Shirk, July 10, 2019; Phone conversation with Nelson Wert, March 2, 2020.

9. Interview with Shaun Seymour, August 8, 2018.

10. Interview with Francisco Jr. and Arlene Good Delgado, April 1, 2020.

11. Horst, Santiago and Siegrist, "Introduction," 8-9.

12. Interview with Paul Martin, June 1, 2017; Interview with Phillip Wert, July 11, 2018.

13. "Polishing English Skills," *Weaver Poultry Lines,* November 11, 1982, 2; "English Class Breaks Barriers," *Weaver Poultry Lines,* March 2, 1983, 1.

14. Interview with Larry Brown, February 18, 2020.

15. Allon Lefever with Mike Yorkey, *Launching the Entrepreneur Ship* (Centennial, CO: WordServe Literary, 2017), 173-174.

CHAPTER 6: THE ERA OF PREPARED FOODS, 1970-1980s

1. *The First Forty Years: A History of Victor F. Weaver, Inc.,* January 1978, Publication No. 118, 8-9; Interview with Melvin Mitchell, April 25, 2017.

2. "Pioneer and Popularizer," *Quick Frozen Foods: The Magazine That Keeps Growing With the Industry,* May 1976, 13,15.

3. Interview with Melvin Mitchell, April 25, 2017; "The First Forty Years," 11.

4. Phone conversation with Michael Good, February 23, 2020.

5. Interview with Melvin Mitchell, April 25, 2017.

6. Lefever, *Launching*, 126,

7. "Future Directions," *Weaver Poultry Lines,* September 1979, 3-5.

8. Family Reflections, July 4, 2017.

9. Interviews with Calvin High, September 19, 2017; December 6, 2019.

10. Interviews with Larry and Janet Newswanger, October 6, 2017; "Reflections." Received by Allan W. Shirk April 5, 2018; Greg Newswanger, "Personal Story," April 5, 2018.

11. Interview with Allon Lefever, April 19, 2020.

12. Interviews with Calvin High, September 19, 2017; December 6, 2019.

13. Interviews with Delbert Seitz, June 7, 2017; March 7, 2018.

14. Interview with Larry Newswanger, February 28, 2020; Larry Newswanger, "Reflections." Received by Allan W. Shirk, February 28, 2020; Eby, John. "Entrepreneurship: A Risk, an Honor, a Challenge," *The Marketplace*, Sept. 1985, 8-9.

15. Phone conversation with Eugene Martin, April 20, 2018.

16. Phone conversation with Nelson Wert, February 21, 2020.

17. Interview with Allon Lefever, April 19, 2020.

18. Interview with Leroy Newswanger, March 23, 2017.

19. "The Pipe," *Entree,* May/June 1980, 12-15.

20. Interview with Leroy Newswanger, March 23, 2017.

21. "What Is Weaver Doing About Pollution?" *The New Holland Clarion*, Vol. XCVIII, July 29, 1971, 1.

22. Interviews with Shaun Seymour, August 9, 2018; March 29, 2018.

CHAPTER 7: AMONG GIANTS: THE CRESTING WAVE OF THE 1980s

1. "Pioneer and Popularizer," *Quick Frozen Foods: The Magazine That Keeps Growing With the Industry,* May 1976, 13,15, 23.

2. Interview with Melvin Mitchell, October 10, 2018.

3. "New President, Board Chairman, Review Corporate Future/Past," *Weaver Poultry Lines,* March 1982, 1.

4. Interview with Melvin Mitchell, April 25, 2017.

5. "Weaver Gains National Exposure," *Weaver Poultry Lines,* May 1978, 3.

6. "Marketing: Expansion Despite Recession," *Weaver Poultry Lines,* 15 September 1983, 1; "Success in the West!" *Weaver Poultry Lines,* September 15, 1983, 7.

7. Interview with Melvin Mitchell, October 16, 2018; "Weaver Expands Operations Southward," *Weaver Poultry Lines,* 7 June 1984.

8. Interview with Keith Stuckey, January 21, 2020.

9. Interview with Allon Lefever, April 22, 2020.

10. Robert A. Weaver Jr. and Associates, Inc. letter, 21 Oct. 1983 to Dale Weaver.

11. Lee Taylor, The Federal Company, letter 18 Jan. 1985 to Dale Weaver.

12. Allon Lefever letter to Dale Weaver, 26 Dec. 1985.

13. Interviews with Allon Lefever, April 19, 2020; April 22, 2020.

14. Lee Taylor, The Federal Company, letter 28 Jan. 1986 to Dale Weaver; Taylor letter to Dale Weaver, 7 Oct. 1986.

15. Interview with Melvin Mitchell, October 25, 2018.

16. Phone conversation with Michael Good, February 23, 2020; Interview with Melvin Mitchell, October 25, 2018.

17. Interview with Allon Lefever, April 19, 2020.

18. Interview with Keith Stuckey, January 21, 2020.

19. Kenneth N. May, Chair and CEO, Holly Farms, letter 19 May 1988 to Victor F. Weaver, Chairman Emeritus.

20. Victor F. Weaver, Inc., 403 South Custer Avenue, New Holland, PA 17557, Notice of Special Meeting of Shareholders, April 25, 1988, 2.

21. Interview with Janet Newswanger, April 25, 2020.

22. Interview with Allon Lefever, April 19, 2020; Interview with Keith Stuckey, January 21, 2020.

23. Interview with Michael Mitchell, Executive Director of the High Center for Family Business at Elizabethtown College, May 22, 2017.

24. Roy. S. Burkholder, *Be Not Conformed to This World: A Narrative History of the Weaverland Mennonites, 1900-1975*, 167-168, 170-171.

25. Family Reflections, July 4, 2017.

26. Interview with Melvin Mitchell, October 16, 2018; Interview with Keith Stuckey, January 21, 2020.

27. Woody Baird, *The WashingtonPost.com*, 24 June 1989, "Holly Farms Accepts Offer of $1.4 Billion from Tyson."

28. Phone conversation with Michael Good, February 23, 2020.

29. Phone conversation with Albert Kunkle, January 17, 2020.

30. Family Reflections, July 4, 2017.

31. Greg Newswanger and Randy Newswanger, "Remembering Grandma, Memorial Service, for Edith M. Weaver, June 26, 2005."

32. Andrea S. Brown, "Security Screening Added after Death-threat Report," *The Lancaster New Era,* September 28, 1993.

33. Interview with Donald Horning, November 23, 2018.

34. Interview with Steve Lindsey, January 31, 2020.

35. Interview with Donald Horning, November 23, 2018.

CHAPTER 8: LEGACY

1. Interview with Michael Mitchell, December 5, 2017.

2. Carole Deck, "New Holland Exhibit Recounts History of Victor F. Weaver, Inc." 8 May 2013. http://lancasteronline.com/elanco/news/new-holland-exhibitrecounts-history-of-victor-f-weaver-inc./article_c89334ac-49c3-593e-ad50-4448102a8203.html.

3. Ed Klimuska, "The Man: Modest Victor F. Weaver Is a Giant in the Poultry Business," *The Lancaster New Era,* 9 Sept. 1986, 1, 8-9.

4. "Pioneer and Popularizer," *Quick Frozen Foods: The Magazine That Keeps Growing With the Industry,* May 1976, 3, 13,15.

5. Lefever, *Launching,* ii.

6. Family Reflections, Camp Hebron, July 4, 2017.

7. Interview with Calvin High, December 6, 2019.

8. Klimuska, 8-9.

Works Cited

BOOKS

Burkholder, Benjamin L. *The Weaver Story.* Unpublished.

Burkholder, Roy S. *Be Not Conformed to This World: A Narrative History of the Weaverland Mennonites, 1900-1975.* Masthof Press, 1998.

Lefever, Allon H. with Mike Yorkey, *Launching the Entrepreneur Ship.* WordServe Literary, 2017.

Stoltzfus, Louise. *As Long as the Grass Grows and Water Flows: The Story of Philhaven.* Philhaven, 2002.

The First Forty Years: A History of Victor F. Weaver, Inc., Victor F. Weaver, Inc. January, 1978.

Weaver, Martin G. *Mennonites of Lancaster Conference.* Mennonite Publishing House, 1931.

———. *Weaverland Settlement, Settlers Graveyard and Its Four Plantations Now Divided Into 45 Farms.* New Holland, 1933.

Weaver, Martin H. and Vera B., and Glori Brubaker. *A Collection of Stories from the Life of Martin H. Weaver.* Lititz, 2004.

Weaver, Raymond H. and Victor F. Weaver. *Descendents of Francis B. Weaver.* June 1981.

PERIODICALS

Baird, Woody. "Holly Farms Accepts Offer of $1.4 Billion from Tyson," *The WashingtonPost.com*, 24 June 1989.

Brown, Andrea S. "Security Screening Added after Death-threat Report," *The Lancaster New Era, 28* September 1993.

Deck, Carole. "New Holland Exhibit Recounts History of Victor F. Weaver, Inc." May 2013. http://lancasteronline.com/elanco/news/new-holland-exhibitrecounts-history-of-victor-f-weaver-inc./article_c89334ac-49c3-593e-ad50-4448102a8203.html

Eby, John. "Entrepreneurship: A Risk, an Honor, a Challenge," *The Marketplace,* Sept. 1985.

Entree, "The Broiler Tradition, a Family," March-April 1990.

Entree, "The Pipe," May/June 1980.

Klimuska, Ed. "The Man: Modest Victor F. Weaver Is a Giant in the Poultry Business," *The Lancaster New Era,* 9 September 1986.

Maisel, Albert Q. "Bedlam 1946: Most U.S. Mental Hospitals Are a Shame and a Disgrace," *Life Magazine*, 6 May 1946.

CORRESPONDENCE

Lefever, Allon H. "Letter to Dale Weaver," 26 Dec. 1985.

Lutz, Clarence E. "Letter of invitation to Victor F. Weaver to attend the Industrial Relations Commission meeting at East Chestnut Street Mennonite Church," 31 Oct. 1953.

May, Kenneth N. Chair and CEO, Holly Farms, "Letter to Victor F. Weaver, Chairman Emeritus, Commending Weaver Family," 19 May 1988.

Newswanger, Greg and Randy Newswanger, "Remembering Grandma, Memorial Service for Edith M. Weaver, 26 June 2005."

Taylor, Lee. "The Federal Company Letter to Dale Weaver," 18 Jan. 1985.

Taylor, Lee. "The Federal Company, Letter to Dale Waver," 28 Jan. 1986.

Taylor, Lee. "Letter to Dale Weaver," 7 Oct. 1986.

Weaver Jr., Robert A. and Associates, Inc. "Letter to Dale Weaver," 21 Oct. 1983.

PROCEEDINGS

Philhaven Hospital Board Minutes, 9 Feb. 1949.

Philhaven Hospital Board Minutes, 19 Oct. 1971.

Weaver, Inc., Victor F. 403 South Custer Avenue, New Holland, Pa. 17557, Notice of Special Meeting of Shareholders, April 25, 1988.

INTERVIEWS

Blank, Lester. 3 April 2020.

Brown, Larry. 18, Feb. 2020.

Brubaker, Robert Sr., and Lois. 11 June 2020.

Delgado, Jr. Francisco and Arlene Delgado. 1 April 2020.

Family Reflections of the United Service Foundation Board. 4 July 2017.

Good, Merle. 26 Dec. 2019.

High, Calvin. 19 Sept. 2017; 6 Dec. 2019.

Horning, Donald. 23 Nov. 2018; 12 March 2019; 31 Jan. 2020.

Lefever, Allon H. 21 Sept. 2017; 19 April 2020; 22 April 2020.

Lindsey, Steve. 31 Jan. 2020.

Martin, Paul. 1 June 2017.

Mitchell, Melvin. 25 April 2017; 5 Dec. 2017; 10 Oct. 2018; 16 Oct. 2018; 25 Oct. 2018.

Mitchell, Michael. 22 May 2017.

Newswanger, Larry and Janet. 30 Sept. 2016; 28 April 2017; 6 Oct. 2017; 24 Jan. 2018; 2 March 2018; 22 April 2019; 20 Dec. 2019; 21 Feb. 2020; 28 Feb. 2020; 21 March 2020; 25 April 2020.

Newswanger, Leroy. 23 March 2017; 26 Feb. 2020.

Pellman, William. 29 Nov. 2016.

Seitz, Delbert. 7 June 2017; 6 Dec. 2019.

Seymour, Shaun. 29 March 2018; 8 Aug. 2018.

Stuckey, Keith. 21 Jan. 2020.

Weaver, Irene M. 2 March 2018.

Weaver, Lamar S. 24 Jan. 2018.

Wert, Philip. 11 July 2018.

Yoder, Jesse. 24 March 2018.

PHONE CONVERSATIONS

Burkholder, Roy S. 10 March 2020; 21 April 2020.

Good, Michael. 22 May 2020.

High, S. Dale. 11 Oct. 2016.

Kunkle, Albert. 17 Jan. 2020.

Martin, Eugene. 20 April 2018; 12 Nov. 2019.

Weaver, Lamar S. 12 Feb. 2020.

Wert, Nelson. 21 Feb. 2020; 2 March 2020.

ELECTRONIC SOURCES

Blank, Lester. "William Lauver." Received by Allan W. Shirk, 3 April 2020.

Glanzer, Tina Hess. "Personal Story." Received by Allan W. Shirk, 10 July 2019.

Lefever, Allon H. "Letter to Dale Weaver." Received by Allan W. Shirk, 22 April, 23 April, 8 May, 2020.

Martin, James. "Serving at Camp Hebron." Received Sept. 8, 2020; phone conversation, Sept. 9, 2020.

Newswanger, Greg. "Personal Story." Received by Allan W. Shirk, 5 April 2018.

Newswanger, Larry. "Reflections." Received by Allan W. Shirk, 5 April 2018; 28 February 2018.

Wert, Melvin. "Personal Story." Received by Allan W. Shirk, 29 November, 2016.

Index

The Author

I have tried to tell Victor and Edith Weaver's story accurately and I take responsibility for any errors of fact or judgment. For anyone whose story I was not aware of, I'm sorry we did not connect.

The Author, Allan W. Shirk. Photo by Ruth Ann Shirk.

I was born in East Earl, Pennsylvania, close to New Holland. As a teenager, I worked for a summer in the Weaver Cut-up Department and enjoyed Weaver poultry products my mother made.

A graduate of Eastern Mennonite College, I received a M.Ed. in Social Studies from the Pennsylvania State University. In 1965 I began teaching social studies at Lancaster Mennonite High School. After teaching 15 years at Western Mennonite School in Oregon, I returned to finish my career at Lancaster Mennonite School, retiring in 2010.

I am married to Ruth Ann Wert Shirk. Our two daughters are Melissa Shirk Jantz (husband, Timothy) and grandson, Ethan; and Beverly Shirk Wilson (husband, Keith) and grandchildren, Owen and Wynona.